# Oh, Scrap!

## FABULOUS QUILTS THAT MAKE THE MOST OF YOUR STASH

  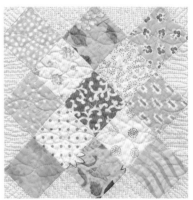

## LISSA ALEXANDER

Martingale®
Create with Confidence

Oh, Scrap! Fabulous Quilts That Make the Most of Your Stash
© 2018 by Lissa Alexander

Martingale®
19021 120th Ave. NE, Ste. 102
Bothell, WA 98011-9511 USA
ShopMartingale.com

Printed in China
23 22 21 20 19 18          8 7 6 5 4 3 2 1

Library of Congress Cataloging-in-Publication Data is available upon request.

ISBN: 978-1-60468-894-8

## MISSION STATEMENT

We empower makers who use fabric and yarn to make life more enjoyable.

## CREDITS

PUBLISHER AND
CHIEF VISIONARY OFFICER
Jennifer Erbe Keltner

CONTENT DIRECTOR
Karen Costello Soltys

MANAGING EDITOR
Tina Cook

ACQUISITIONS EDITOR
Karen M. Burns

TECHNICAL EDITOR
Nancy Mahoney

COPY EDITOR
Sheila Chapman Ryan

PRODUCTION MANAGER
Regina Girard

COVER AND
INTERIOR DESIGNER
Adrienne Smitke

STUDIO PHOTOGRAPHER
Brent Kane

LOCATION PHOTOGRAPHER
Adam Albright

ILLUSTRATOR
Sandy Huffaker

SPECIAL THANKS
*Thanks to Julie Smiley of Des Moines, Iowa, for allowing us to photograph this book in her home.*

## Dedication

To my mom for teaching me to work with my hands.

To my sister for believing in me.

To the rest of my family for being able to
sleep to the hum of my sewing machine.

# Contents

# PREFACE:
## Musings on the History of Scrap Quilting

### By Barbara Brackman

Scrap quilts are as old as American patchwork. One of the earliest surviving American quilts was made for 27-year-old Anna Tuels of Massachusetts by her mother, who appliquéd the year 1785 in the center. Anna's mother, the wonderfully named Experience Taylor Tuels, stitched the medallion quilt mostly of triangles cut from dozens of silks, cottons, wools, and linens and bordered the composition with a bright pink wool.

An undated early American treasure is in the Smithsonian Institution's collection. The Copp family medallion contains well over one hundred different pieces of 18th-century and early 19th-century fabrics in its stars and squares. Where did that scrap bag come from? Some of the Connecticut Copps were in the dry goods business. They advertised imported goods: "elegant light and dark Chintzes and Calicoes." Perhaps the Copp girls were inclined to save a small swatch of every fabric that came in the shop. Just a small scrap: some of the stars in the quilt finish to 3" square.

We see early references to the term "scrap quilt" too, although not quite so early as those first patchwork quilts. An 1858 grammar book defined it: "A scrap quilt has all kinds of pieces." The earliest reference I've found to the idea, if not the term itself, was in the records of a Massachusetts fair in 1837. Lucy Bowler entered two quilts. Press at the time wrote: "In one, every square is a different style." County fairs 150 years ago sometimes mentioned entries and prizes for scrap quilts.

*"Scrap quilts are as old as American patchwork."*

For several years in the 1860s, Pennsylvania's Greene County fair awarded $2 prizes in four categories:

+ Best White Quilt
+ Best Fancy Quilt
+ Best Scrap Quilt
+ Best Patch (Appliqué) Quilt

Were scrap quilts considered less valuable than fancy or appliquéd quilts? There seems to have been argument—some of it rather heated. An 1883 farm magazine divided the world into opposite camps. On one side: those who "dote on bed quilts, spend all their spare time cutting and putting together pieces, beg quantities of calico scraps from the neighbors...." The other group "denounce pieced quilts and declare that...star and angles make a hideous bed-covering." The editor advocated a middle ground. Don't bother the neighbors, and keep busy but not obsessed.

In various magazines, readers weighed in on the topic: "Nothing...is neater in my opinion than a neat scrap quilt to say nothing of economy. I save every scrap left over from my dresses and aprons...."

In 1874, a fan of scrap quilts wrote she could not defend buying "costly material just to cut up and sew together." On the other hand, "Who has not calico scraps? Even Mrs. Grant [the President's wife], I presume, has calico dresses.... What could be nicer than a neatly made, pretty, calico patchwork quilt, although she need not use it at the White House unless she wishes." Julia Grant, who did make at least one quilt but apparently had some difficulty finishing it, did not comment.

Martha Haggard achieved newspaper celebrity in 1898 with a widely circulated story about her accomplishments with the needle. This "industrious old lady" counted 112 "Scrap quilts, pieced, containing from 500 to almost 63,000 separate pieces" over the past 30 years. That last quilt of 63,000 patches is in the collection of the Helen F. Spencer Museum of Art at the University of Kansas.

Many believe that quilts made from small scraps grow out of scarcity of fabric or cash, but quilters realize a stash of any variety requires an investment. Scrap quiltmakers from Experience Tuels, the Copp family, and Martha Haggard to scrappers today realize it's cheaper to make a quilt from a few large pieces than hundreds of tiny ones. Small pieces waste fabric in the seams. I've lifted Martha Haggard's masterpiece of 63,000 pieces and it's the heaviest quilt I've ever met. She estimated that there were 36 yards of cloth in the top (about six times the usual yardage).

Hard times like the Great Depression of the 1930s certainly encouraged a thrifty approach to reusing material, but the scrap look, then as now, is a choice. One could solicit scraps from the neighbors and beg for samples at the dry

*Ad from* The Farmer's Wife *magazine, 1927.*

## "A scrap quilt has all kinds of pieces."

goods store, but Depression-era quiltmakers who wanted variety in their Grandmother's Flower Garden and Double Wedding Ring quilts could buy scraps by the pound.

The men who kept accounts at fabric mills and clothing factories long realized that a fabric mill's trash might be a scrap piecer's treasure. Silk mills helped create the Crazy quilt fad in the 1880s with packages of factory cutaways. Women's magazines often contained ads such as: "Silk and Velvet Pieces for Crazy Quilts— Assorted colors, pretty patterns. Bound to please you. Large package. 16 cents."

Rather than discarding leftovers, mills marketed them to quilters, using a variety of terms. In 1922 the dry goods store in Winnsboro, South Carolina, advertised "5-pound. quilt bundles" for 98 cents. The editor of *Comfort* magazine bought remnants from a necktie factory and packaged them as "Sadie's Silken

Shower of Satin Samples," which could be purchased with coins or by mailing in magazine subscriptions.

About 1930, Capper's *Household Magazine* offered "Quilting Material Free" as subscription premiums. Readers could send 25 cents in stamps for "a cellophane wrapped package containing 25 new and different pieces of print material in all shades of the rainbow."

The 1934 Sears catalog offered two packages of cotton scraps for quilters. "Washfast Quilt Patches Rainbow Lots of Prints, Plains" for 59 cents and "World's Fair Quilt Patches, Fresh Bright Prints; a Few Plain Colors" for 22 cents. Another Sears ad sold "Rag Bundles" with ideas for sewing projects.

So no matter if you beg, snip, or buy your scraps, remember that you're following a great American tradition.

# Scrap Quilts: The New Vintage

As someone who's been quilting for 30 years, and using precuts for the last 10, I've made my fair share of scrap quilts and have learned so much in the process. My background was in quilt retail before I became the marketing director at Moda Fabrics. By watching and listening to customers to see what they liked and why things worked (or didn't), I built my knowledge of making scrap quilts and I'm happy to share with you what I've learned.

Because making scrap quilts requires using a lot of different fabrics (something beginner quilters haven't amassed yet), I'm assuming you're more of an intermediate quilter—or you're on your way! So you won't find lots of basic quiltmaking information here. What you will find are my tips and suggestions for making scrap quilts that sing.

Whether your goal is to finally get to the bottom of your scrap basket or raid your stash to cut patches from bigger pieces of fabrics, I'll share my tips on what makes a good scrap quilt (and no, it's not including *everything but the kitchen sink)* so you can achieve amazing results regardless of how big the fabric pieces were that you started with.

To me, scrap quilts are the new vintage quilts. I love that they can look old and remind you of something your grandma might have made. On the other hand, they can be totally fresh looking. Whichever look you're going for, each scrap quilt will be unique because we each have our own fabric stashes, favorite colors, and tastes.

My hope is that you'll learn some new ways of looking at colors and prints that will help you choose fabrics so you can assemble scrap quilts everyone in your family will love—starting with any of the dozen patterns in this book!

Let's get scrappy,

*~ Lissa*

# Precuts and Stashes and Scraps—Oh My!

As we learned from quilt historian Barbara Brackman in her preface, not all scrap quilts are literally made from scraps. Not even those made a century ago. Scrap quilts have captured our fascination and we love to make them. But we might use fabrics from our stashes, swap pieces with friends, or break open a brand-new bundle of precut fabrics to make them. That said, sometimes mixing many fabrics together to make a cohesive design can seem intimidating—you don't want to end up with a hodgepodge. So let's avoid the "everything but the kitchen sink" approach and learn how to mix fabrics effectively. Many of the quilts in this book, while having dozens or even more than 100 fabrics, are very limited in color palette. Let's take a closer look at color, value, scale, and all the things that go into making a beautiful scrap quilt.

## Glossary of Intimidating Color Terms

No color workshop is complete without them!

I love color but have always been a bit intimidated by the color wheel and all the terms that go with it, like *primary, secondary,* and *tertiary.* (Tertiary?) That said, it's helpful to know some of these words and what they mean so that you can put your finger on what works and why. When choosing fabrics for scrap quilts, I rely mainly on three factors: value, scale, and density. But let's start with the words that relate to color.

**Hue.** A fancy word for color. Most quilters store fabrics by color, but you never hear a quilter say, "I store my fabric by hue." Hue has more to do with pure color in the world of paint and isn't all that important to fabric.

**Tint.** A tint is a color with white added to lighten it. If you add white to orange, the result is peach.

**Shade.** A shade is the opposite of a tint—it's color with black added to deepen it. Add black to orange and you get rust.

**Tone.** Tone is when you add gray to a color. It mutes the brightness of the color. Which brings us to...

**Chroma.** This is how bright a color is.

**Value.** The value of a color is how dark or light it is, ranging from light to medium to dark. In print fabrics, the background color most likely determines its value. When making scrap quilts, I look at value more than color, as it's the value placement that makes a quilt design work. Where you put the dark, medium, and light fabrics defines the stars or churn dashes or crosses in your blocks. It's important to remember that value is relative.

*Value is relative, meaning a fabric can appear to be dark or light depending on which fabric it's placed next to.*

**Scale.** Scale relates to the size of the patterned design on the fabric, not to the color. But it's a term we use when talking about combining fabrics. Scale is an important consideration when choosing fabrics for a quilt, whether you're shopping in a store or from your stash. If you're always drawn to small-scale florals, then your stash will be full of many similar types of prints. And using only prints of the same scale can result in a quilt that is ho-hum.

*Incorporating a variety of print sizes makes for more interesting compositions.*

**Density.** Density refers to the closeness of the design. Some prints have lots of space between the patterns while others are packed tightly together throughout the fabric. Using fabrics with varying densities is what forces your eyes to slow down and view the individual pieces. Have you ever been at a quilt show and seen a group of people gathered around a quilt longer than the others? Yes, it's usually the grand-prize winner, but quite often it's a winner because there's a variety in fabric density—the stop and start, the yin and yang. Density also plays into that all-important concept of value.

*Print density ranges from very loose to quite compact, looking from left to right.*

## Start with a Two-Color Scrap Quilt

If you're like me and a bit overwhelmed by the whole color-wheel thing, I recommend starting simply, with a basic color scheme of two colors that appeal to you. When I teach classes on color, I actually start by using just black and white. Without color, it's easier to determine the relative *value*. But instead of black and white, let's pick two colors.

These two colors can be your favorites, or two that you've not worked with in the past. Chose red and green, blue and pink, or whatever two colors speak to you.

Be liberal in your interpretation of color. Let's say red is one of your two colors. Don't overlook pink, burgundy, or coral. There's cherry red, tomato red, plum red. Don't second-guess whether these will go together. Add them to your pile of reds. There will be time to eliminate some of them later. As noted fabric and quilt designer Jen Kingwell says, "It's easier to make a quilt with 100 different fabrics than it is to make one with ten." In the end, everyone who views your quilt will see it as a red quilt; they won't question why some of the reds are more pink and others are more orange.

Not all of the fabrics in a scrap quilt need to be your favorites. We can't all be the prom queen, after all! That doesn't mean less appreciated fabrics can't work well in a scrap quilt when blended with other prints of the same color. So dig through your stash and pull out all the possible choices.

## Swatch Cards

As you page through this book, you'll see swatch cards for many of the projects. These are close-up photos of fabrics I used in the quilts so that you can see just how much I stretched the limits when it comes to red prints or green prints or low-volume prints. The reason we like looking at scrap quilts is that all those prints—the colors, the scales, the values—add interest. The variety of fabrics contributes complexity to even the simplest of quilt designs without necessarily adding more colors. Consider making a swatch card for your next quilt. It helps you see not just how well your choices go together, but it also helps you determine what may be missing.

For an example of limited-color scrap quilts, turn to Sherbet Stars on page 45 or Kismet on page 73. Remember, only the number of *colors* is limited—not the number of *fabrics*.

## Precuts—the New Scraps

As the marketing director for Moda Fabrics, I'm fortunate to have a large stash of fabrics to work with. But not everyone does. And when Moda prints a new line of fabric, we realize that not everyone can buy every fabric in a line. So we offer precut bundles in a variety of sizes so that quilters like you can take home one of everything. You can choose Jelly Rolls, which are 2½" × 44" strips, or charm squares, which come in a standard 5" size or a 2½" mini size. And then there's my favorite, the Layer Cake, which gives you 42 squares that are each 10" × 10". I find Layer Cakes are a perfect foundation for scrap quilts because you get decent-sized chunks of fabric to work with, and there are 42 of them!

As fun as precut bundles are, I rarely use all of the fabrics from one bundle in a single quilt. I like to pick and choose, then I put the remainders in my stash and mix and match them with other fabrics for another scrap quilt. Precuts are a handy way to build a stash for scrap quilting. But if you feel precut bundles are a bit too matchy-matchy, mix them up and use them with fabrics from other lines, other designers, and other fabrics you already have in your stash.

## Storing Fabrics with Scrap Quilts in Mind

Notice how we're talking about making scrap quilts, but we haven't even mentioned the terms "scrap basket" or "scrap bin" once? Of course we all create scraps when we quilt, but when it comes to making a scrap quilt, I rarely dig through a basket to find a little piece of this or a chunk of that. Like most quilters, I store my fabrics by color. But I also store my leftovers (partial fat quarters, Jelly Roll strips with a portion cut off, what's left of a Layer Cake square after I've cut a chunk out of it) by color too.

One of my favorite ways to store scraps is to fold them and store them in acrylic refrigerator bins, according to color. These sit side-by-side on my shelf, they're handy to pull out and sort through when I'm planning a quilt, and the fabrics stay flat and tidy—not in a jumbled heap as they would in a true scrap basket.

## Your Best Scrap Quilt Ever

Armed with a few simple principles regarding value, scale, and density, I hope you'll enjoy making any of the dozen patterns in this book. You don't need to follow my color schemes. Use your favorite colors to make these patterns uniquely yours. If, like most of us, you find it hard to see beyond the colors used, for most of the projects you'll also find an illustrated version of an alternate colorway—simply to help you to see that quilt patterns can work well in completely different ways.

My hope is that you'll enjoy dreaming up your own scrappy colors schemes. And when you do, please share photos of your quilts and tag them with *#OhScrap!* I'd love to see your results.

# Plus Marks the Spot

I've always loved the Swiss army knife. Not only as a handy tool, but also for its classic red color with a white cross, the coat of arms of Switzerland. The versatility of the cross motif makes it perfect for a scrap quilt. Here, the anchoring point is the royal blue at the center of each cross or plus sign. It's the strongest color in the quilt, so the busier prints don't stand out much in comparison. Don't be afraid to use some busy prints to give this project a vintage feel.

**FINISHED QUILT: 34½" × 42½"  |  FINISHED BLOCK: 6" × 6"**

## Materials

*Yardage is based on 42"-wide fabric.*

+ ¼ yard *total* of assorted dark blues for block centers (A)
+ ½ yard *total* of assorted medium and dark prints for blocks (B)
+ ½ yard *total* of assorted light prints for blocks (C)
+ ⅞ yard of white solid for background
+ ½ yard of navy dot for binding
+ 2⅜ yards of fabric for backing*
+ 41" × 49" piece of batting

*\*If the backing fabric is at least 41" wide after washing and trimming off the selvages, you'll only need 1⅜ yards of fabric.*

## Cutting

**From the A fabrics, cut a *total* of:**
20 squares, 2½" × 2½"

**From the B fabrics, cut a *total* of:**
80 squares, 2½" × 2½"

**From the C fabrics, cut a *total* of:**
80 squares, 2½" × 2½"

**From the white solid, cut:**
11 strips, 2½" × 42"; crosscut into:
    2 strips, 2½" × 38½"
    2 strips, 2½" × 34½"
    4 strips, 2½" × 30½"
    15 rectangles, 2½" × 6½"

**From the navy dot, cut:**
5 strips, 2½" × 42"

squares together into rows. Join the rows to make a block. Make 20 blocks, measuring 6½" square.

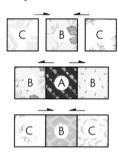

Make 20 blocks, 6½" × 6½".

## Instant Scraps

Don't have a lot of scraps? Start with mini charms (packs of 2½" squares) from some of your favorite fabric designers and you'll be able to whip up these Nine Patches in a snap. Substitute a Bella solid Jelly Roll for the sashing-fabric yardage, and you'll save even more time!

## Making the Blocks

The blocks are made up of A, B, and C squares. To create the plus signs, I used the same color family for each block's B squares. You can do the same, or you could instead place colors randomly. Press the seam allowances in the directions indicated by the arrows.

Arrange four C squares, four B squares, and one A square in three rows as shown. Sew the

## Assembling the Quilt Top

**1.** Join three white 2½" × 6½" rectangles and four blocks to make a block row. Make five rows that measure 6½" × 30½", including the seam allowances.

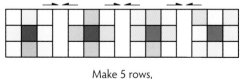

Make 5 rows, 6½" × 30½".

**2.** Sew the white 2½" × 30½" strips and block rows together to make the quilt-top center. The quilt top should measure 30½" × 38½", including the seam allowances.

**3.** Sew the white 38½"-long strips to opposite sides of the quilt top. Sew the white 34½"-long strips to the top and bottom of the quilt top to complete the border. The quilt top should measure 34½" × 42½".

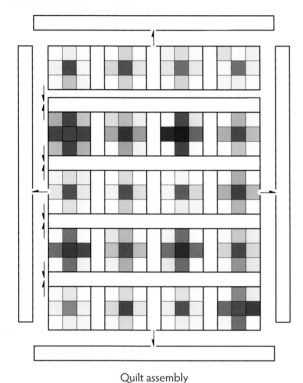

Quilt assembly

## Finishing the Quilt

For more details on any of the finishing steps, go to ShopMartingale.com/HowtoQuilt to download free illustrated information.

**1.** Layer the backing, batting, and quilt top; baste.

**2.** Hand or machine quilt. The quilt shown is machine quilted with an allover pumpkin seed pattern.

**3.** Sew the navy 2½"-wide strips together end to end with 45° seams to make the binding. Fold this long strip in half lengthwise with wrong sides together and press. Use the long strip to bind the quilt.

## Alternate Colorway

Plus Marks the Spot is, at its most basic, a Nine Patch quilt with sashing. No triangles, no tricky seam intersections, and no foundation piecing required. That makes it a quilt that's totally achievable for beginners. But most beginners don't have a large stash of fabrics or scraps to work with. Instead, you can choose a favorite color (in this case blue) and select several fat quarters or fat eighths of assorted blues to piece the blocks. Notice that the blocks in this alternative colorway don't all have light corners, as in the original quilt. Just mix up the 2½" squares randomly to make a totally loveable Baby Blues quilt.

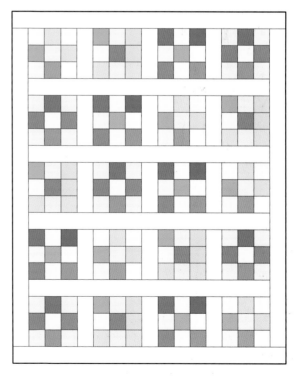

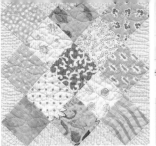

# Izzy Squared

The block in this quilt is a variation of the traditional Album block, which is often referred to as a Granny Square since it's reminiscent of a crocheted granny-square afghan. I call it Izzy Squared because Izzy is what my grandkids call me. (My niece Kennedy couldn't say "Lissa," so somehow I became "Izzy" and it stuck.) I'm good with that, because I want to be a cool grandmother and not a "Granny"! This quilt is so much fun to make, it's offered it in three different sizes to suit anyone!

**FINISHED CRIB QUILT: 43¼" × 53½"** | **FINISHED THROW QUILT: 63¾" × 74"**
**FINISHED QUEEN QUILT: 84¼" × 84¼"** | **FINISHED BLOCK: 8½" × 8½"**

## Materials

*Yardage is based on 42"-wide fabric. Materials are given for 3 different sizes.*

### CRIB QUILT

+ ¼ yard *total* of assorted red prints for block centers (A)
+ ½ yard *total* of assorted prints for blocks (B)
+ 1¾ yards *total* of assorted prints for blocks and sashing (C)
+ 1 yard of white print for background (D)
+ ½ yard of orange diagonal stripe for binding
+ 2⅞ yards of fabric for backing
+ 50" × 60" piece of batting

### THROW QUILT

+ ¼ yard *total* of assorted red prints for block centers (A)
+ 1 yard *total* of assorted prints for blocks (B)
+ 3½ yards *total* of assorted prints for blocks and sashing (C)
+ 1⅞ yards of white print for background (D)
+ ⅔ yard of orange diagonal stripe for binding
+ 4½ yards of fabric for backing
+ 70" × 80" piece of batting

### QUEEN QUILT

+ ½ yard *total* of assorted red prints for block centers (A)
+ 1½ yards *total* of assorted prints for blocks (B)

*Continued on page 22*

*Continued from page 21*

- 5¼ yards *total* of assorted prints for squares and sashing (C)
- 2¾ yards of white print for background (D)
- ⅞ yard of orange diagonal stripe for binding
- 7¾ yards of fabric for backing
- 93" × 93" piece of batting

# Cutting

*Cutting is given for 3 sizes.*

## CRIB QUILT

**From the A fabrics, cut a *total* of:**
20 squares, 2½" × 2½"

**From the B fabrics, cut a *total* of:**
80 squares, 2½" × 2½"

**From the C fabrics, cut a *total* of:**
49 rectangles, 2¼" × 9"
160 squares, 2½" × 2½"

**From the D fabric, cut:**
5 strips, 4" × 42"; crosscut into 40 squares, 4" × 4". Cut each square into quarters diagonally to yield 160 side triangles.
5 strips, 2¼" × 42"; crosscut into 70 squares, 2¼" × 2¼". Cut *40 of the squares* in half diagonally to yield 80 corner triangles.

**From the orange diagonal stripe, cut:**
6 strips, 2½" × 42"

## THROW QUILT

**From the A fabrics, cut a *total* of:**
42 squares, 2½" × 2½"

**From the B fabrics, cut a *total* of:**
168 squares, 2½" × 2½"

**From the C fabrics, cut a *total* of:**
97 rectangles, 2¼" × 9"
336 squares, 2½" × 2½"

**From the D fabric, cut:**
10 strips, 4" × 42"; crosscut into 84 squares, 4" × 4". Cut each square into quarters diagonally to yield 336 side triangles.
9 strips, 2¼" × 42"; crosscut into 140 squares, 2¼" × 2¼". Cut 84 *of the squares* in half diagonally to yield 168 corner triangles.

**From the orange diagonal stripe, cut:**
8 strips, 2½" × 42"

## QUEEN QUILT

**From the A fabrics, cut a *total* of:**
64 squares, 2½" × 2½"

**From the B fabrics, cut a *total* of:**
256 squares, 2½" × 2½"

**From the C fabrics, cut a *total* of:**
144 rectangles, 2¼" × 9"
512 squares, 2½" × 2½"

**From the D fabric, cut:**
15 strips, 4" × 42"; crosscut into 128 squares, 4" × 4". Cut each square into quarters diagonally to yield 512 side triangles.
13 strips, 2¼" × 42"; crosscut into 209 squares, 2¼" × 2¼". Cut *128 of the squares* in half diagonally to yield 256 corner triangles.

**From the orange diagonal stripe, cut:**
10 strips, 2½" × 42"

## Leftover Precuts

Many of my scrap quilts start with leftovers from precuts, as I rarely use the entire bundle of precuts. I subcut the leftovers into sizes I use a lot, such as 2½" squares. That said, don't be so efficient that you cut all your scraps into small squares. In this quilt, the sashing strips are 9" long, and they too are cut from scraps.

## Making the Blocks

Using the same color family for the four inner B squares and a different color family for the eight outer C squares gives some color structure to the layout of each block. You can follow this layout or use a random color placement for the C squares. Refer to the photo above and the block diagram on page 24 for color placement throughout. You'll need 20 blocks for the crib quilt, 42 blocks for the throw quilt, and 64 blocks for the queen quilt. Press the seam allowances in the directions indicated by the arrows.

**1.** For each block, select one A square, four B squares, eight C squares, eight D side triangles, and four D corner triangles. Sew D side triangles to opposite sides of a C square to make a unit. Make two units.

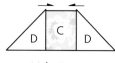

Make 2 units.

**2.** Join C squares to opposite sides of a B square. Sew a D side triangle to each end of the row to make a unit. Make two units.

Make 2 units.

**3.** Sew a C and a B square to *each* side of an A square to make a unit that's 2½" × 10½".

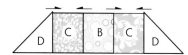

Make 1 unit.

**4.** Join the units from steps 1–3 to make the center unit.

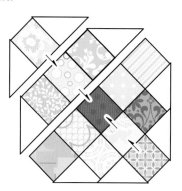

Make 1 unit.

**5.** Sew a D corner triangle to each corner to complete the block. Make 20 blocks that measure 9" square for the crib quilt.

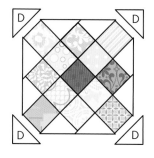

Make 20 blocks,
9" × 9".

## Things in Common

At first glance you might think that the blocks in this quilt are quite different from one another. Some use just two colors, some have a third color that makes a cross in the center of the block, some are bold, and some recede. But to keep them unified in some way so that the design works well, all the blocks have a red center square. And all the sashing cornerstones and background pieces are the same white fabric. Those may not be the parts of the quilt that stand out to you, but they're the bits that help make a cohesive design.

**6.** Repeat steps 1–5 to make 42 blocks if you're making the throw quilt or 64 blocks if you're making the queen quilt.

## Assembling the Crib Size

**1.** Join five D squares and four C rectangles to make a sashing strip. Make six sashing strips that measure 2¼" × 43¼", including the seam allowances.

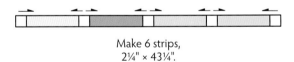

Make 6 strips,
2¼" × 43¼".

**2.** Join five C rectangles and four blocks to make a block row. Make five rows that measure 9" × 43¼", including the seam allowances.

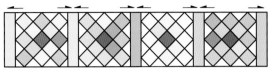

Make 5 rows,
9" × 43¼".

**3.** Join the sashing strip and block rows, alternating them as shown in the crib-quilt assembly diagram below. The quilt top should measure 43¼" × 53½".

**4.** Stitch around the perimeter of the quilt top, ⅛" from the outer edges, to lock the seams in place.

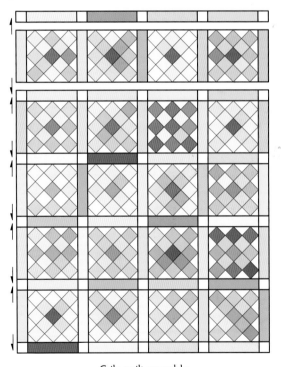

Crib-quilt assembly

## Assembling the Throw Size

**1.** Join seven D squares and six C rectangles to make a sashing strip. Make eight sashing strips that measure 2¼" × 63¾", including the seam allowances.

**2.** Join seven C rectangles and six blocks to make a block row. Make seven rows that measure 9" × 63¾", including the seam allowances.

**3.** Join the sashing strip and block rows, alternating them as shown in the throw-quilt assembly diagram below. The quilt top should measure 63¾" × 74".

**4.** Stitch around the perimeter of the quilt top, ⅛" from the edges, to lock the seams in place.

## Assembling the Queen Size

**1.** Join nine D squares and eight C rectangles to make a sashing strip. Make nine sashing strips that measure 2¼" × 84¼", including the seam allowances.

**2.** Join nine 2¼" × 9" C rectangles and eight blocks to make a block row. Make eight rows that measure 9" × 84¼", including the seam allowances.

**3.** Join the sashing strip and block rows, alternating them as shown in the queen quilt assembly diagram. The quilt top should measure 84¼" × 84¼".

**4.** Stitch around the perimeter of the quilt top, ⅛" from the edges, to lock the seams in place.

Throw

Queen

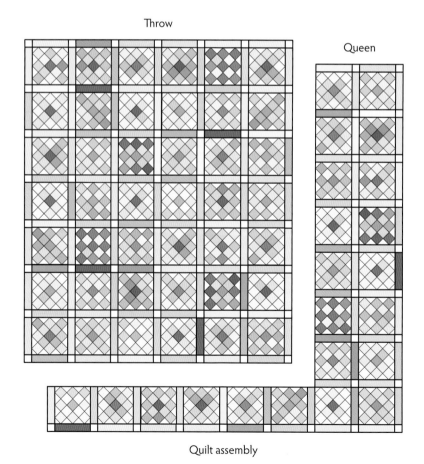

Quilt assembly

## Finishing the Quilt

For more details on any of the finishing steps, go to ShopMartingale.com/HowtoQuilt to download free illustrated information.

**1.** Layer the backing, batting, and quilt top; baste.

**2.** Hand or machine quilt. The quilt shown is machine quilted with a four-petal flower in each small square and ribbon candy loops in the sashing strips.

**3.** Sew the orange striped 2½"-wide strips together end to end with 45° seams to make the binding. Fold this long strip in half lengthwise with wrong sides together and press. Use the long strip to bind the quilt.

## Alternate Colorway

For something completely different, imagine Izzy Squared stitched from a more neutral palette of tans, browns, rusts, taupes, and grays. Wouldn't this be a perfect throw-sized quilt for the leather chair in your den?

### Swatch Cards

For this quilt, I chose fabrics that were predominantly medium-value prints. My colors ranged from yellow to green to blue, and from pink to coral to red. I also tossed in some gray and lavender, but to make them all work, no one color was exceedingly darker than the others.

# Awesome Land

I named this quilt after an episode of one of my favorite television shows, *Modern Family*. It was a Halloween episode where the family patriarch, Jay, was tired of being the ugly guy because he never had a costume. Like Jay, orange is often considered the ugly color. I think orange gets a bad rap. When I first started buying antique quilts, I always bought the orange ones; they were all I could afford. And if you shop for orange fabrics all year long, and not just in October, you can get ones that don't have Halloween spiders, witches, or skulls on them. Give orange a chance!

**FINISHED QUILT: 70½" × 93"  |  FINISHED BLOCK: 6" × 6"**

## Materials

*Yardage is based on 42"-wide fabric.*

+ 2⅝ yards *total* of assorted orange, red, gold, and coral prints for blocks, inner border, and binding (A)

+ 3⅛ yards *total* of assorted cream, tan, and light gray prints for blocks and sashing (B)

+ 1¾ yards *total* of assorted black and charcoal prints for blocks and cornerstones (C)

+ ½ yard of medium gray print for middle border (D)

+ 2¼ yards of white-with-black print for outer border (E)

+ 6⅝ yards of fabric for backing

+ 79" × 101" piece of batting

## Cutting

**From the A fabrics, cut a *total* of:**
108 squares, 2½" × 2½" (54 sets of 2 matching squares)
54 rectangles, 2½" × 6½" (Match 1 rectangle to each set of squares.)
2½"-wide strips in varying lengths, enough to total 650"

**From the B fabrics, cut a *total* of:**
216 squares, 2½" × 2½" (54 sets of 4 matching squares)
30 rectangles, 2½" × 6½"
34 rectangles, 2" × 2½"
123 rectangles, 2" × 6½"
4 squares, 2½" × 2½"

*Continued on page 30*

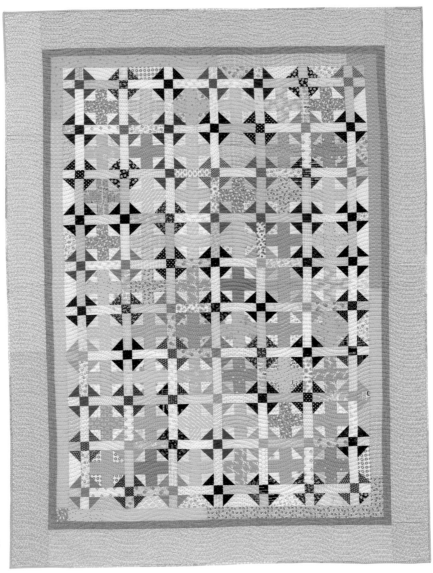

*Quilted by Abby Latimer*

*Continued from page 29*

**From the C fabrics, cut a *total* of:**

280 squares, 2½" × 2½" (70 sets of 4 matching squares)

70 squares, 2" × 2" (Match 1 square to each set of 4 matching 2½" squares.)

**From the D fabric, cut:**

8 strips, 1¾" × 42"

**From the E fabric, cut:**

10 strips, 7" × 42"

## Making the Blocks

A design wall or flat surface where you can lay out the blocks is necessary for this project. Press the seam allowances in the directions indicated by the arrows.

**1.** Lay out two A squares and one A rectangle, all matching, and four matching 2½" B squares. Sew the B squares to opposite sides of each A square to make the top and bottom block rows.

Sew the top and bottom rows to opposite sides of the A rectangle to make a unit. Make 54 units that measure 6½" square.

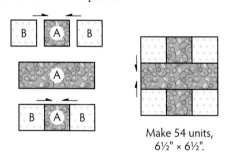

Make 54 units,
6½" × 6½".

**2.** Layer 2½" B and C squares right sides together. Sew diagonally across the B square from corner to corner. Trim away the excess corner fabric, leaving a ¼" seam allowance. Make four different half-square-triangle units that measure 2½" square.

Make 4 units,
2½" × 2½".

## Making a Planned Scrap Quilt

One of the reasons I like making scrap quilts is not only to use up existing fabrics, but also to do some mindless sewing. If I need to stop to cook dinner, answer the phone, or take the kids to a ballgame, I can pick up right where I left off. But to make this design work, it wasn't just about randomly sewing together a lot of orange and gray fabrics. It was about creating a secondary design of gray Shoofly blocks. You see, the main block is an orange plus sign, with scrappy gray corners. But each corner needs to be the same fabric as the corners of the blocks next to it to create the design. Not exactly mindless, but not hard either. You just have to plan each row as you go so that the corner triangles match the adjacent triangles.

**3.** On a design wall, lay out the units from step 1, placing 2" × 6½" B rectangles between the units. Place a half-square-triangle unit and matching 2" C square in each corner of the quilt. Place a 2" C square between the B rectangles to make sashing rows. Then add the 2½" × 6½" and 2" × 2½" B rectangles around the perimeter as shown.

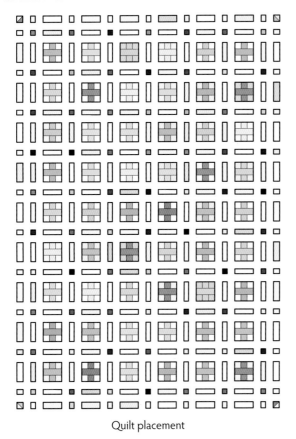

Quilt placement

**4.** To create the secondary Shoofly blocks, place 2½" C squares on the corners of each step 1 unit and the 2½" × 6½" B rectangles. The 2½" squares and 2" square should all match. Pin the squares in place on each unit and rectangle, right sides together. *You should have four different C prints on each step 1 unit, as shown in step 5, above right.*

**5.** Sew diagonally across a C square from corner to corner as shown. Flip the square back over the corner with the right side facing up and press. Trim away the excess corner fabric, leaving a ¼" seam allowance. In the same way, sew a C square to each corner of the unit to complete a block. Return the block to the correct place in the quilt layout. Make 54 blocks that measure 6½" square.

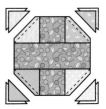

Make 54 blocks,
6½" × 6½".

**6.** For the border units, sew a C square on the left end of a 2½" × 6½" B rectangle, stitching diagonally across the square from corner to corner as shown. Flip the square back over the corner with the right side facing up and press. Trim away the excess corner fabric, leaving a ¼" seam allowance. In the same way, sew a C square to the other end of the rectangle to complete a sashing unit. Return the unit to the correct place in the quilt layout. Make 30 units that measure 2½" × 6½".

Make 30 units,
2½" × 6½".

# Assembling the Quilt Top

**1.** Sew together the pieces in each row as shown, making sure to work on one row at a time. Return the row to its correct position in the quilt layout. Join the rows to complete the quilt top. The quilt top should measure 51" × 73½", including the seam allowances.

**2.** Sew the 2½"-wide A strips together end to end using a straight seam to make a 260"-long strip. From the pieced strip, cut two 73½"-long strips and two 55"-long strips. Sew the 73½"-long strips to opposite sides of the quilt top. Sew the 55"-long strips to the top and bottom of the quilt top to complete the inner border. The quilt top should measure 55" × 77½", including the seam allowances.

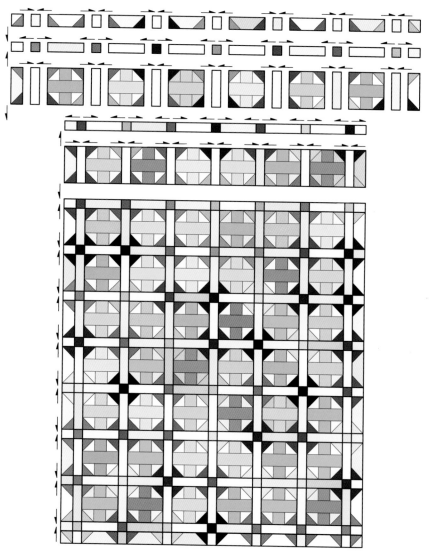

Quilt assembly

**3.** Sew the 1¾"-wide D strips together end to end using a diagonal seam. From the pieced strip, cut two 77½"-long strips and two 57½"-long strips. Sew the 77½"-long strips to opposite sides of the quilt top. Sew the 57½"-long strips to the top and bottom of the quilt top to complete the middle border. The quilt top should measure 57½" × 80", including the seam allowances.

**4.** Sew the 7"-wide E strips together end to end using a diagonal seam. From the pieced strip, cut two 80"-long strips and two 70½"-long strips. Sew the 80"-long strips to opposite sides of the quilt top. Sew the 70½"-long strips to the top and bottom of the quilt top to complete the outer border. The quilt should measure 70½" × 93".

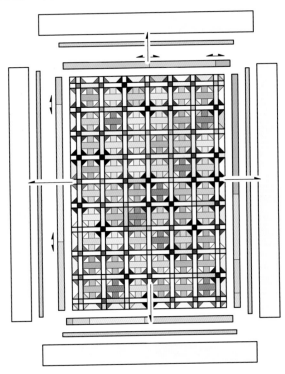

Adding borders

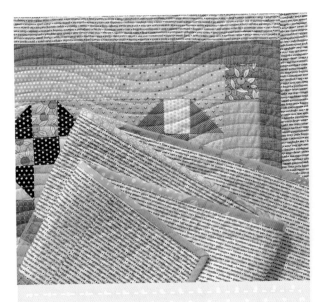

## *Scrappy to the End*

Notice that in this quilt, the middle and outer borders are each made of one fabric. But the inner orange border is made from scraps, as is the binding, adding a bit of whimsy right up to the edge!

## Finishing the Quilt

For more details on any of the finishing steps, go to ShopMartingale.com/HowtoQuilt to download free illustrated information.

**1.** Layer the backing, batting, and quilt top; baste.

**2.** Hand or machine quilt. The quilt shown is machine quilted with horizontal serpentine lines spaced about ½" apart.

**3.** Sew the remaining 2½"-wide A strips together end to end with 45° seams to make the binding. Fold this long strip in half lengthwise with wrong sides together and press. Use the long strip to bind the quilt.

## Swatch Cards

When planning a two-color scrap quilt, you need a lot of fabrics in each colorway. For this quilt, it meant a lot of oranges. Notice, however, that my palette ranges from coral to orange to butterscotch. I call this the clash factor. Don't match colors too closely, or the quilt will be one dimensional.

## Alternate Colorway

Hard as I try, I just can't make everyone love orange. What's your favorite color? Use it as the quilt's main color and chose a second color to go with it that will recede, such as gray or taupe. You'll have a quilt with a secondary pattern in a color you'll enjoy.

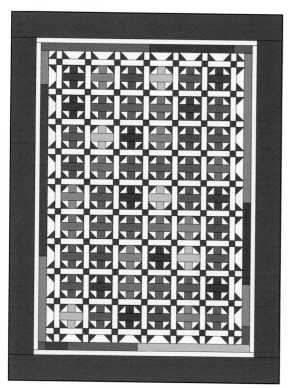

# Surrounded

Surrounded is probably my all-time favorite quilt. Why? Because it broke me out of my comfort zone. I'd started to notice that the scraps left from my Moda precuts were always the light-colored midsize to large prints, what are known as "low-volume" fabrics. They didn't fit the science of how I planned my color schemes. So I challenged myself to create a low-volume quilt. This quilt first appeared in *American Patchwork & Quilting* magazine's first quilt-along series, and many quilters have shared their versions with me. I hope you will as well. Use the hashtag #ohscrapsurrounded.

**FINISHED QUILT: 75½" × 93½"** | **FINISHED BLOCK: 15" × 15"**

## Materials

*Yardage is based on 42"-wide fabric.*

+ 7 yards *total* of assorted light prints for blocks and sashing (A)
+ 1¾ yards *total* of assorted red, pink, and orange prints for blocks and sashing (B)
+ 1⅛ yards *total* of assorted yellow, blue, green, and aqua prints for blocks (C)
+ ⅞ yard of blue dot for binding
+ 7 yards of fabric for backing
+ 84" × 102" piece of batting

## Cutting

**From the A fabrics, cut a *total* of:**
49 rectangles, 3½" × 15½"
80 rectangles, 3½" × 5½"
160 rectangles, 2½" × 3½"
240 rectangles, 1½" × 2½"
680 squares, 1½" × 1½"

**From the B fabrics, cut a *total* of:**
80 squares, 2½" × 2½" (20 sets of 4 matching squares)
420 squares, 1½" × 1½" (20 sets of 21 matching squares; match each set to a set of 4 matching 2½" squares.)
150 squares, 1½" × 1½" (30 sets of 5 matching squares)

*Continued on page 38*

*Continued from page 37*

**From the C fabrics, cut a *total* of:**

240 squares, 1½" × 1½" (20 sets of 12 matching squares)

160 rectangles, 1½" × 2½" (20 sets of 8 matching rectangles; match each set to a set of 12 matching 1½" squares.)

**From the blue dot, cut:**

10 strips, 2½" × 42"

## It's All About the Value

If you're having a hard time determining what's a "low-volume" print and what isn't, remember—it's all about the value. And value is relative. If the prints you're using for the chain portion of the block are bright and bold (like some of the reds and deeper blues in my quilt), you can probably tell pretty easily that the lighter colors you've selected for the background will be light enough.

However, if you're using some lighter-value prints for the chain, such as the golds, yellows, and pinks like I've used, you need to make sure your low-volume prints are low enough! Simply audition your fabrics next to the lightest of your B and C fabric groups to make sure you can still see enough contrast to make the chain stand out.

As you can see in my quilt on page 39, some of the chain colors are rather close to the background values, but overall the chain stands out against the background and the shifts in value make your eyes dance around the quilt top.

## Making the Blocks

Each block is made with one fabric B print, one fabric C print, and an assortment of fabric A prints. For each block, you'll need the following pieces:

+ Fabric A: 28 squares, 1½"; eight rectangles, 2½" × 3½"; 12 rectangles, 1½" × 2½"; and four rectangles, 3½" × 5½"

+ Fabric B: 21 squares, 1½", and four squares, 2½"; all matching

+ Fabric C: 12 squares, 1½", and eight rectangles, 1½" × 2½"; all matching

Instructions are for making one block; repeat to make a total of 20 blocks. Press the seam allowances in the directions indicated by the arrows.

**1.** Lay out two fabric A and two 1½" fabric B squares in two rows. Sew the squares together into rows. Join the rows to make a four-patch unit. Make four matching units that measure 2½" square, including the seam allowances.

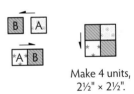

Make 4 units,
2½" × 2½".

**2.** Lay out four fabric A, three fabric B, and two fabric C squares in three rows. Sew the squares together into rows. Join the rows to make a nine-patch unit. Make four matching units that measure 3½" square, including the seam allowances.

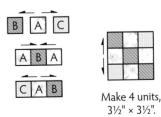

Make 4 units,
3½" × 3½".

**3.** Lay out one four-patch unit, one nine-patch unit, and two 2½" × 3½" A rectangles in two rows. Sew the pieces together into rows. Join the rows to make a corner unit. Make four matching units that measure 5½" square, including the seam allowances.

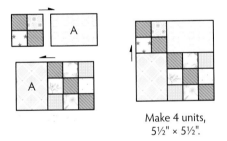

Make 4 units,
5½" × 5½".

**4.** Join two 1½" × 2½" A rectangles and one C square to make a unit. Make four matching units that measure 1½" × 5½", including the seam allowances.

Make 4 units,
1½" × 5½".

**5.** Join two 1½" × 2½" C rectangles and one A square to make a unit. Make four matching units that measure 1½" × 5½", including the seam allowances.

Make 4 units,
1½" × 5½".

**6.** Sew a step 4 unit to a step 5 unit. Make four matching units that measure 2½" × 5½", including the seam allowances.

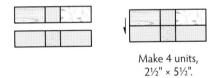

Make 4 units,
2½" × 5½".

**7.** Sew a step 6 unit to a 3½" × 5½" A rectangle to make a side unit. Make four matching units that measure 5½" square, including the seam allowances.

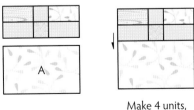

Make 4 units,
5½" × 5½".

**8.** Lay out four 2½" B squares, four 1½" × 2½" A rectangles, and one 1½" B square in three rows. Sew the squares and rectangles together into rows. Join the rows to make a center unit. Make one unit that measures 5½" square, including the seam allowances.

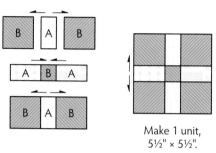

Make 1 unit,
5½" × 5½".

**9.** Lay out four corner units, four side units, and one center unit in three rows. Sew the units together into rows. Join the rows to complete a block that measures 15½" square, including the seam allowances.

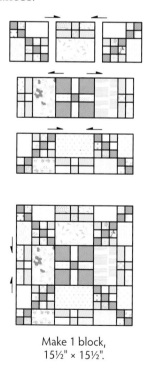

Make 1 block,
15½" × 15½".

**10.** Repeat steps 1–9 to make a total of 20 blocks.

## Making the Sashing Blocks

Lay out five B and four A squares in a nine-patch arrangement. Sew the squares together into rows. Join the rows to make a sashing block. Make 30 blocks that measure 3½" square, including the seam allowances.

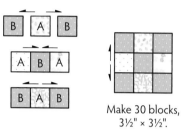

Make 30 blocks,
3½" × 3½".

## Assembling the Quilt Top

**1.** Join five sashing blocks and four 3½" × 15½" A rectangles to make a sashing row. Make six rows that measure 3½" × 75½", including the seam allowances.

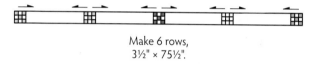

Make 6 rows,
3½" × 75½".

**2.** Join five 3½" × 15½" A rectangles and four blocks to make a block row. Make five rows that measure 15½" × 75½", including the seam allowances.

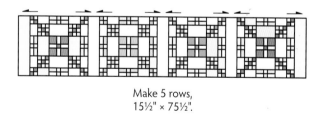

Make 5 rows,
15½" × 75½".

**3.** Join the sashing rows and block rows, alternating them as shown in the quilt assembly diagram below to complete the quilt top, which should measure 75½" × 93½".

**4.** Stitch around the perimeter of the quilt top, ⅛" from the outer edges, to lock the seams in place.

## Finishing the Quilt

For more details on any of the finishing steps, go to ShopMartingale.com/HowtoQuilt to download free illustrated information.

**1.** Layer the backing, batting, and quilt top; baste.

**2.** Hand or machine quilt. The quilt shown is machine quilted with a feather wreath motif in the background and straight lines through the diagonal chains of squares.

**3.** Sew the blue dot 2½"-wide strips together end to end with 45° seams to make the binding. Fold this long strip in half lengthwise with wrong sides together and press. Use the long strip to bind the quilt.

Quilt assembly

## Swatch Cards

Take a look at the low-volume prints in the swatch card, right. Notice that they aren't all white or cream. They have visible prints like dots and words. And they have color. Together, the colors and prints add up to low-volume impact!

## Alternate Colorway

Surrounded is my take on a traditional Burgoyne Surrounded quilt pattern, named for a British general who fought (and lost when his regiment was surrounded) in the American Revolutionary War. This design is reminiscent of the woven coverlets that were popular during that time period. Coverlets were often woven in red and white. Imagine this quilt stitched from a hundred different red prints, rather than just one!

# Sherbet Stars

I've made this pattern multiple times in a variety of colorways. Each of the nine blocks is made the same way—eight-pointed stars, with each point made of nine diamonds. It's the value placement that varies in each block, making this quilt look as if it were made from nine different star blocks. If value is something that seems challenging to you, this quilt offers the chance to explore the possibilities.

**FINISHED QUILT: 81¾" × 81¾"  |  FINISHED BLOCK: 21¾" × 21¾"**

## Materials

*Yardage is based on 42"-wide fabric.*

+ 3¼ yards *total* of assorted dark pink, coral, and orange prints for blocks (A)
+ 5 yards *total* of assorted light pink and cream prints for blocks and outer border (B)
+ ¾ yard of pink print for binding
+ 7½ yards of fabric for backing
+ 90" × 90" piece of batting

*The blocks are scrappy, but by varying the placement of the lightest and darkest strips in the strip sets on pages 46 and 48, you can change the secondary pattern within each star. Play with your strip sets and watch different variations emerge. We show two different blocks, but there are variations in all the blocks.*

## Cutting

**From the A fabrics, cut a *total* of:**
30 strips, 2" × 42"*
16 squares, 5⅜" × 5⅜"; cut each square in half
    diagonally to yield 32 small triangles
16 squares, 7¼" × 7¼"; cut each square in half
    diagonally to yield 32 large triangles

**From the B fabrics, cut a *total* of:**
24 strips, 2" × 42"
20 squares, 5⅜" × 5⅜"; cut each square in half
    diagonally to yield 40 small triangles
20 squares, 7¼" × 7¼"; cut each square in half
    diagonally to yield 40 large triangles
8½"-wide strips in varying lengths, to total 320"

**From the pink print, cut:**
9 strips, 2½" × 42"

*\*These can be pieced randomly from shorter strips to total 42"-long strips.*

*Quilted by Natalia Bonner*

## Making Block 1

Press the seam allowances in the directions indicated by the arrows.

**1.** Join three fabric A strips along their long edges to make a strip set. Make 10 strip sets that measure 5" × 42".

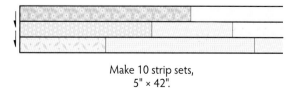

Make 10 strip sets,
5" × 42".

**2.** Using a rotary cutter and a ruler with 45° markings, align the 45° line with an edge of a strip set as shown. Trim the end of the strip set.

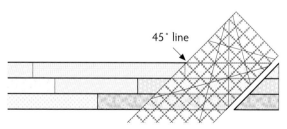

45˚ line

**3.** Rotate the strip set 180°. Measure 2" from the freshly cut end of the strip set and cut a

2"-wide segment. Repeat, cutting 2" segments from the fabric A strip sets for a total of 120 segments.

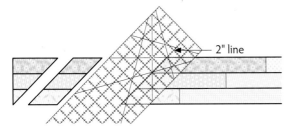

Cut 120 segments.

**4.** Sew three A segments together as shown to make a diamond unit. Make 20 units. To form a dark star in the center of the block (as in the center block of the quilt), be sure to have a darker print at the bottom-left diamond position.

Make 20.

**5.** Sew a small B triangle to right side of a diamond unit. Sew a large B triangle to the top of the unit to make a triangle unit. Make 20 units.

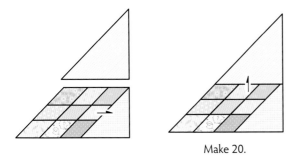

Make 20.

**6.** Join three A segments as shown to make a reversed diamond unit. Make 20 units.

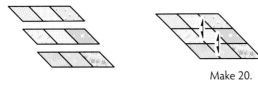

Make 20.

## Flip before You Rip

When you sew the units together and notice that the seam intersections don't look perfect, flip before you rip. It could save you a lot of time and trouble. What do I mean by that? If you have a gap where two units should have met up perfectly, your first instinct may be to rip open the seam and restitch it to look better. Sometimes, however, simply flipping the seam allowance to the opposite side shifts the heft of the fabric and makes the two units look like they fit together perfectly. The photos above show the same unit. I didn't resew the seemingly imperfect unit; I simply flipped the seam allowance to face the opposite direction, and the result was a perfect seam intersection!

**7.** Sew a small B triangle to left side of a reversed diamond unit. Sew a large B triangle to the top of the unit to make a reversed triangle unit. Make 20 units.

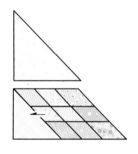
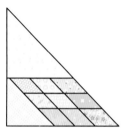

Make 20.

**8.** Join triangle units from steps 5 and 7 along their long edges to make a quadrant. Make 20 quadrants that measure 11⅜" square.

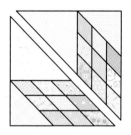
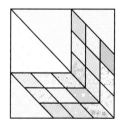

Make 20 quadrants, 11⅜" × 11⅜".

**9.** Lay out four quadrants in a four-patch arrangement. Sew the quadrants together into rows. Join the rows to complete one block. Make five blocks that measure 22¼" square.

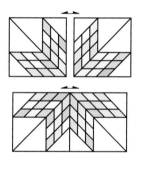
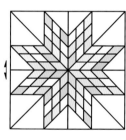

Block 1.
Make 5 blocks, 22¼" × 22¼".

## Making Block 2

**1.** Join three fabric B strips along their long edges to make a strip set. Make eight strip sets that measure 5" × 42". If you'd like to make a dark star in the center of the block, be sure to use a darker fabric in the bottom-left corner of the strip set.

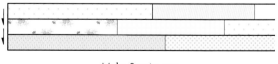

Make 8 strip sets, 5" × 42".

**2.** Rotate the strip set 180°. Using a rotary cutter and a ruler with 45° markings, align the 45° line with an edge of a strip set and trim the end of the strip set.

**3.** Then rotate the strip set 180° again. Measure 2" from the freshly cut end of the strip set and cut a 2"-wide segment. Repeat, cutting 2" segments from the fabric B strip sets for a total of 96 segments.

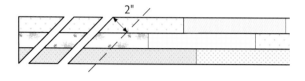

Cut 96 segments.

**4.** Sew three B segments together as shown to make a diamond unit. Make 16 units and 16 reversed units.

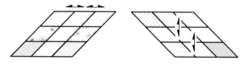

Make 16 of each.

**5.** Sew a small A triangle to right side of a diamond unit. Sew a large A triangle to the top of the unit to make a triangle unit. Make 16 units.

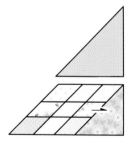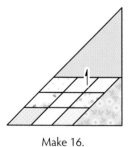

Make 16.

**6.** Sew a small A triangle to left side of a reversed diamond unit. Sew a large A triangle to the top of the unit to make a reversed triangle unit. Make 16 units.

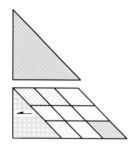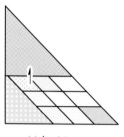

Make 16.

**7.** Join triangle units from steps 4 and 5 along their long edges to make a quadrant. Make 16 quadrants that measure 11⅜" square.

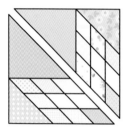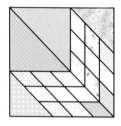

Make 16 quadrants,
11⅜" × 11⅜".

**7.** Lay out four quadrants in a four-patch arrangement. Sew the quadrants together into rows. Join the rows to complete one block. Make four blocks that measure 22¼" square.

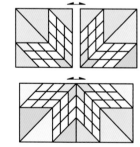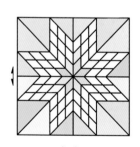

Block 2.
Make 4 blocks,
22¼" × 22¼".

## Assembling the Quilt Top

**1.** Lay out the blocks in three rows of three blocks each, alternating them as shown in the quilt assembly diagram below. Sew the blocks together into rows. Join the rows to complete the quilt-top center, which should measure 65¾" square, including the seam allowances.

**2.** Sew the 8½"-wide B strips together end to end using a straight seam. From the pieced strip, cut two 65¾"-long strips and two 81¾"-long strips. Sew the 65¾"-long strips to opposite sides of the quilt top. Sew the 81¾"-long strips to the top and bottom of the quilt top to complete the border. The quilt should measure 81¾" square.

## Finishing the Quilt

For more details on any of the finishing steps, go to ShopMartingale.com/HowtoQuilt to download free illustrated information.

**1.** Layer the backing, batting, and quilt top; baste.

**2.** Hand or machine quilt. To get a highly textured look, quilter Natalia Bonner used a light pink thread that subtly contrasts the creams, oranges, and deeper pinks among the fabrics.

**3.** Sew the pink 2½"-wide strips together end to end with 45° seams to make the binding. Fold this long strip in half lengthwise with wrong sides together and press. Use the long strip to bind the quilt.

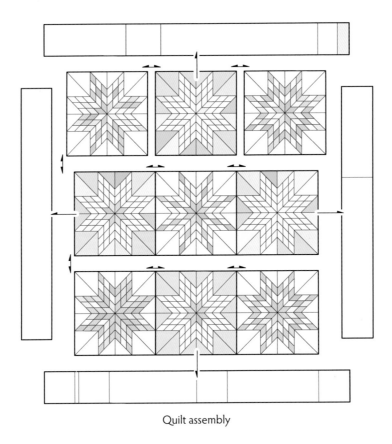

Quilt assembly

## Swatch Cards

Don't be afraid to stretch the boundaries. Everyone who has seen this quilt has called it pink. Including me. But look at the range of prints I used (right): pale shell pink, bubble-gum pink, peach, even a bit of butterscotch. Whatever main color you use, stretch beyond the conventional.

## Alternate Colorway

I hear you. Pink isn't for everyone. But this quilt design can be. With nine blocks and your favorite colors, you can mix and match them to your heart's delight. You have nine opportunities to play with the color and value placement to make each star different in appearance. Here, I've selected shades of blue and gold for a heavenly option. What colors will you choose?

# Old Meets New

For this romantic quilt made using many floral prints, I wanted to showcase some spectacular large-scale prints. That's why I ended up making 17"-square blocks. The corner triangles just begged to be made from big, bold prints. Adding 8"-wide borders, each one from a different fabric, is a perfect ending to this feminine quilt.

**FINISHED QUILT: 75½" × 75½"** | **FINISHED BLOCK: 17" × 17"**

## Materials

*Yardage is based on 42"-wide fabric.*

+ ¾ yard *total* of assorted light prints (cream, tan, blue, gray, and pink) for blocks (A)
+ 2⅜ yards *total* of assorted medium prints (tan, brown, blue, and pink) for blocks (B)
+ 1⅛ yards *total* of assorted dark brown prints for blocks and triangle border (C)
+ 2¼ yards *each* of 4 large-scale light prints for blocks and borders (D)
+ ⅔ yard of brown print for binding
+ 6⅞ yards of fabric for backing
+ 82" × 82" piece of batting

## Cutting

**From the *lengthwise* grain of *each* D fabric, cut:**
1 strip, 8" × 79" (4 total)

**From the A fabrics and remaining D fabrics, cut a *total* of:**
16 strips, 2" × 18"
18 squares, 5¼" × 5¼" (9 sets of 2 matching squares); cut each square into quarters diagonally to yield 8 matching triangles (72 total)
38 squares, 3⅞" × 3⅞"

**From the B fabrics, cut a *total* of:**
18 squares, 9⅜" × 9⅜" (9 sets of 2 matching squares); cut each square in half diagonally to yield 4 matching triangles (36 total)
144 squares, 2½" × 2½" (18 sets of 8 matching squares)
4 squares, 4½" × 4½"

*Continued on page 54*

*Continued from page 53*

**From the C fabrics, cut a *total* of:**

18 squares, 5¼" × 5¼" (9 sets of 2 matching squares); cut each square into quarters diagonally to yield 8 matching triangles (72 total)

5 squares, 4½" × 4½"

38 squares, 3⅞" × 3⅞"

**From the brown print for binding, cut:**

9 strips, 2½" × 42"

## Making the Blocks

Press the seam allowances in the directions indicated by the arrows.

**1.** Sew two pairs of contrasting 2½" B squares together as shown to make a four-patch unit. Make nine sets of four matching units (36 total). The units should measure 4½" square, including the seam allowances.

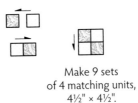

Make 9 sets
of 4 matching units,
4½" × 4½".

**2.** Join two A and two C triangles as shown to make an hourglass unit. Make nine sets of four matching units (36 total). The units should measure 4½" square, including the seam allowances.

Make 9 sets of
4 matching units,
4½" × 4½".

**3.** Lay out four matching four-patch units, four matching hourglass units, and one 4½" B or C square in three rows as shown. Sew the pieces together into rows. Join the rows to complete a center unit. Make nine units that measure 12½" square, including the seam allowances. Note that in one block (middle row, right), the four-patch units are rotated so that the lighter color is in the block corners.

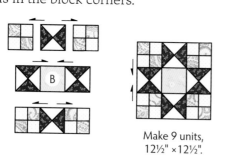

Make 9 units,
12½" ×12½".

**4.** Using four matching B triangles, center and sew the triangles on each side of a center unit to complete a block. Make nine blocks that measure 17½" square, including the seam allowances.

Make 9 blocks,
17½" ×17½".

## Making the Triangle Border

**1.** Layer an A square on top of a 3⅞" C square, right sides together. Draw a diagonal line from corner to corner on the top square. Sew ¼" from each side of the marked line. Cut the units apart on the marked line to make two half-square-triangle units. Make a total of 76 units that measure 3½" square.

Make 76 units,
3½" × 3½".

**2.** Sew 18 half-square-triangle units together to make a side border. Repeat to make a second side border. The borders should measure 3½" × 54½", including the seam allowances.

Make 2 borders, 3½" × 54½".

**3.** Sew 20 half-square-triangle units together to make the top border. Repeat to make the bottom border. The borders should measure 3½" × 60½", including the seam allowances.

Make 2 borders, 3½" × 60½".

## Assembling the Quilt Top

**1.** Referring to the quilt assembly diagram on page 56, lay out the blocks in three rows of three blocks each. Sew the blocks together into rows. Join the rows to complete the quilt-top center, which should measure 51½" square, including the seam allowances.

**2.** Join the 2" × 18" A strips end to end using a diagonal seam to make a long strip. From the long strip, cut two inner-border strips 51½" long and sew them to opposite sides of the quilt top.

**3.** From the remaining long strip, cut two 54½"-long inner-border strips. Sew the strips to the top and bottom of the quilt top, which should now measure 54½" square, including the seam allowances.

**4.** Sew the 54½"-long triangle borders to opposite sides of the quilt top. Sew the 60½"-long triangle borders to the top and bottom of the quilt top. The quilt top should measure 60½" square, including the seam allowances.

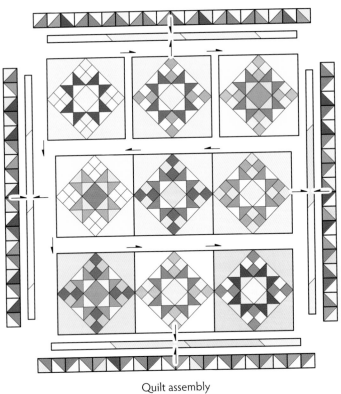

Quilt assembly

## Perfect Mitered Ending

Notice that even the outer border on this quilt is scrappy. Each side of the quilt uses a different print, but the border frames the quilt nicely because each side of the border is similar in value to the others.

For the perfect finishing touch, be sure to miter the corners of the outer border. When blocks are set on point, your quilt has lots of diagonal lines, and the mitered corners on the border create a picture-frame effect that continues the diagonal theme.

If you love big romantic prints, this is an excellent way to showcase them.

**5.** Center and pin a 79"-long A strip on one side of the quilt top. Sew the strip to the quilt top, starting ¼" from the top edge and stopping a ¼" from the bottom edge. *Do not* trim the excess strip. Repeat, sewing the remaining A strips to the other sides of the quilt.

**6.** To miter each corner, fold the quilt top with right sides together, aligning the adjacent edges of the border. Draw a diagonal line from the previously sewn seam to the outer edges of the border. Sew on the marked line. Trim the excess border strip, leaving a ¼" seam allowance. Repeat to miter the remaining corners.

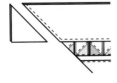

Align 45° mark on stitching line.

## Finishing the Quilt

For more details on any of the finishing steps, go to ShopMartingale.com/HowtoQuilt to download free illustrated information.

**1.** Layer the backing, batting, and quilt top; baste.

**2.** Hand or machine quilt. The quilt shown is machine quilted with swirls and loops in the blocks and a feather motif in the outer border.

**3.** Sew the brown 2½"-wide strips together end to end with 45° seams to make the binding. Fold this long strip in half lengthwise with wrong sides together and press. Use the long strip to bind the quilt.

## Alternate Colorway

Soft shades of blues and greens come together effortlessly in a soothing color scheme. Use the darkest hues for the star points and pieced border and the lighter tones for a restful background. Even with a limited color palette such as this, the more fabrics the better.

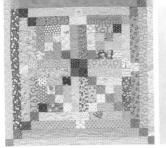

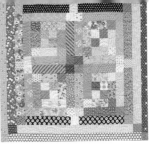

# Splendid Scraps

Two very talented ladies, Pat Sloan and Jane Davidson, created an entire quilting community by inviting designers to create 6" quilt blocks that would then be shared online in a project called the Splendid Sampler. I was fortunate to be a part of this group, and my block was called Starting Point. When learning anything new, there's always a starting point. Sometimes it's like jumping off a cliff and seeing where you land. For this scrappy quilt, I joined four of the Starting Point blocks and framed them, and the quilt grew from there, just as my community of quilting friends has grown.

**FINISHED QUILT: 54½" × 72½"  |  FINISHED BLOCK: 18" × 18"**

## Materials

*Yardage is based on 42"-wide fabric.*

+ ⅞ yard *total* of assorted gray prints for blocks (A)
+ ⅝ yard *total* of assorted light prints for blocks (B)
+ 4⅔ yards *total* of assorted bright prints (red, pink, blue, green, and yellow) for blocks (C)
+ ⅝ yard of red dot for binding
+ 3½ yards of fabric for backing
+ 61" × 79" piece of batting

## Cutting

**From the A fabrics, cut a *total* of:**
432 squares, 1½" × 1½"

**From the B fabrics, cut a *total* of:**
336 squares, 1½" × 1½"

**From the C fabrics, cut a *total* of:**
48 rectangles, 1½" × 16½"
48 rectangles, 1½" × 14½"
96 rectangles, 1½" × 6" (48 sets of 2 matching rectangles)
192 rectangles, 1½" × 4½"
192 rectangles, 1½" × 2½"

**From the red dot, cut:**
7 strips, 2½" × 42"

*Quilted by Maggi Honeyman*

## Making the Blocks

Press the seam allowances in the directions indicated by the arrows.

**1.** Sew two A and two B squares together to make a four-patch unit. Make 48 units that measure 2½" square, including the seam allowances.

Make 48 units,
2½" × 2½".

**2.** Lay out two A and two B squares, four 1½" × 2½" C rectangles, and one four-patch unit as shown. Sew the pieces together into rows. Join the rows to make a unit. Make 48 units that measure 4½" square, including the seam allowances.

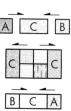

Make 48 units,
4½" × 4½".

**3.** Lay out two A and two B squares, four 1½" × 4½" C rectangles, and one step 2 unit as shown. Sew the pieces together into rows. Join the rows to make a unit. Make 48 units that measure 6½" square, including the seam allowances.

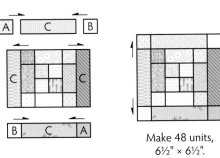

Make 48 units, 6½" × 6½".

**4.** Lay out four step 3 units in two rows, making sure the A squares meet in the center. Sew the units together into rows. Join the rows to make a unit. Make 12 units that measure 12½" square, including the seam allowances.

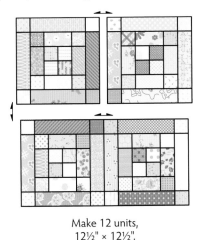

Make 12 units, 12½" × 12½".

**5.** Join a B square and two matching 1½" × 6" C rectangles to make a unit. Make 48 units that measure 1½" × 12½", including the seam allowances.

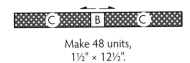

Make 48 units, 1½" × 12½".

## Everything but the Kitchen Sink!

Don't be afraid to use all types of scraps in a quilt like this. I started with a basic color plan, and if the fabric was the right color, I used it. Don't think you have to use just florals or stick only with geometrics. Look closely and you'll see florals, geometrics, polka dots (you can never have too many), checks, tic-tac-toe motifs, leaping dogs, grumpy cat faces, and anything else that fit with my color plan. The strips are narrow enough that none of the prints stand out as an oddball. But when you look closely, you may get a chuckle or two.

**6.** Lay out four A squares, four step 5 units, and one step 4 unit in three rows. Sew the squares and units together into rows. Join the rows to make a unit. Make 12 units that measure 14½" square, including the seam allowances.

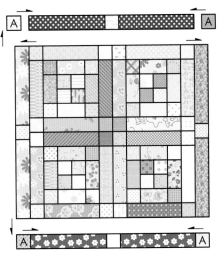

Make 12 units, 14½" × 14½".

**7.** Sew four A squares, four 1½" × 14½" C rectangles, and one step 6 unit together into three rows. Join the rows to make a unit. Make 12 units that measure 16½" square, including the seam allowances.

**8.** Sew four A squares, four 1½" × 16½" C rectangles, and one step 7 unit together into three rows. Join the rows to complete a block. Make 12 blocks that measure 18½" square, including the seam allowances.

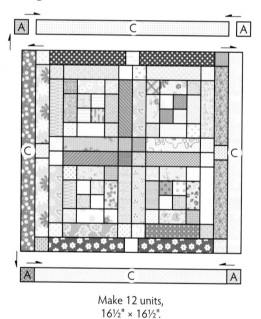

Make 12 units,
16½" × 16½".

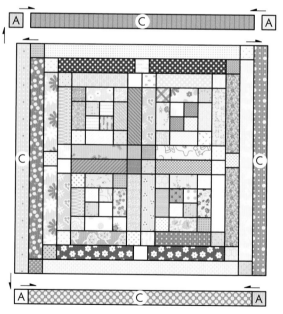

Make 12 blocks,
18½" × 18½".

## Jump In!

Don't let the quantity of pieces intimidate you. You don't need to cut everything at once. Just jump in and get started, one block at a time. You may want to make a single 18" block for a floor pillow. Or make four blocks for a 36"-square baby quilt. Then again, you may have so much fun that you'll end up with a big quilt like mine!

## Assembling the Quilt Top

**1.** Lay out the blocks in four rows of three blocks each. Sew the blocks together into rows. Join the rows to complete the quilt top. The quilt top should measure 54½" × 72½".

**2.** Stitch around the perimeter of the quilt top, ⅛" from the edges, to lock the seams in place.

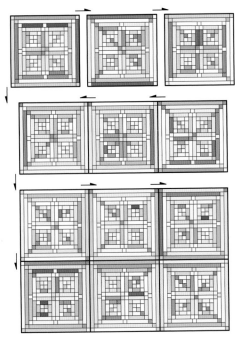

Quilt assembly

## Finishing the Quilt

For more details on any of the finishing steps, go to ShopMartingale.com/HowtoQuilt to download free illustrated information.

**1.** Layer the backing, batting, and quilt top; baste.

**2.** Hand or machine quilt. The quilt shown is machine quilted with a feather motif in each block.

**3.** Sew the red 2½"-wide strips together end to end with 45° seams to make the binding. Fold this long strip in half lengthwise with wrong sides together and press. Use the long strip to bind the quilt.

## Alternate Colorway

The original quilt contains many bright colors, reined in with a bit of gray. If you'd like to pull in the reins even more, consider a three-color quilt, like this red-white-and-blue version. It'll be perfect for the patriots in your life.

# Stair Steps

Some of the best things happen by accident—including this quilt. An evening of what I call mindless therapeutic sewing included chain sewing squares together. I didn't notice until I started pressing that I had subconsciously created patterns using the brighter colors of bubblegum pinks, cheddars, teals, and blues. This pattern would translate nicely into any family of colors, and assorted charm packs or mini-charm packs work great.

**FINISHED QUILT: 80½" × 96½"  |  FINISHED BLOCK: 16" × 16"**

## Materials

*Yardage is based on 42"-wide fabric.*

+ 5¼ yards *total* of assorted dark prints for blocks (A)
+ 3¼ yards *total* of assorted light prints for blocks (B)
+ ½ yard *total* of assorted gold prints for blocks (C)
+ ½ yard *total* of assorted pink prints for blocks (D)
+ ⅓ yard *total* of assorted blue prints for blocks (E)
+ ⅓ yard *total* of assorted purple prints for blocks (F)
+ ⅞ yard of dark red print for binding
+ 7½ yards of fabric for backing
+ 89" × 105" piece of batting

## Cutting

**From the A fabrics, cut a *total* of:**
984 squares, 2½" × 2½"

**From the B fabrics, cut a *total* of:**
60 rectangles, 4½" × 8½"
60 squares, 4½" × 4½"

**From the C fabrics, cut a *total* of:**
64 squares, 2½" × 2½"

**From the D fabrics, cut a *total* of:**
72 squares, 2½" × 2½"

**From the E fabrics, cut a *total* of:**
48 squares, 2½" × 2½"

**From the F fabrics, cut a *total* of:**
32 squares, 2½" × 2½"

**From the dark red print, cut:**
10 strips, 2½" × 42"

## Making the Blocks

All the blocks are assembled the same way but have specific color placement for the fabric C–F squares. Start by making all the A units, which are scrappy four patches using the fabric A squares. Then add the fabric B squares and rectangles to make the B units. After that, working on one type of block at a time to keep the color chain in order, make blocks 1–5 as follows. Press the seam allowances in the directions indicated by the arrows.

### A UNITS

Lay out four fabric A squares in a four-patch arrangement. Sew the squares together to make unit A. Make 208 units that measure 4½" square, including the seam allowances.

Make 208 A units,
4½" × 4½".

## *Chain PRESSING*

We've all heard of chain piecing. But do you also do chain *pressing?* While it's probably good to get up from the machine and press intermittently, I like to take all the units to the ironing board at once and press them while they're still attached. I call this chain pressing. It lets me see which way the units need to be pressed so that adjoining ones can be pressed in opposite directions and won't need to be re-pressed later.

## B UNITS

Sew each B square to an A unit. Make 60. Sew a B rectangle to the bottom of the unit to make unit B. Make 60 units that measure 8½" square, including the seam allowances. Note that about half of the units have the A unit on the left and half on the right. In addition, in 19 of the blocks, I substituted the B rectangle with two B squares, just for fun!

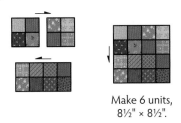

Make a total of 60 B units,
8½" × 8½".

## BLOCK 1

**1.** Lay out four A units in two rows. Sew the units together into rows. Join the rows to make a unit. Make six units that measure 8½" square, including the seam allowances.

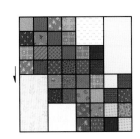

Make 6 units,
8½" × 8½".

**2.** Lay out two step 1 units and two B units in two rows. Sew the units together to complete block 1. Make three blocks that measure 16½" square, including the seam allowances.

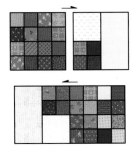

Block 1.
Make 3 blocks,
16½" × 16½".

## BLOCK 2

**1.** Lay out two A and two C squares as shown. Sew the squares together to make a four-patch unit. Make 32 units that measure 4½" square, including the seam allowances.

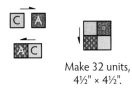

Make 32 units,
4½" × 4½".

**2.** Lay out two step 1 units and two A units in two rows as shown to make a gold diagonal chain. Sew the units together into rows. Join the rows to make a unit. Make 16 units that measure 8½" square, including the seam allowances.

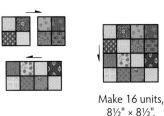

Make 16 units,
8½" × 8½".

**3.** Lay out two step 2 units and two B units in two rows as shown to make a gold diagonal chain. Sew the units together to complete block 2. Make eight blocks that measure 16½" square, including the seam allowances.

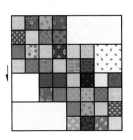

Block 2.
Make 8 blocks,
16½" × 16½".

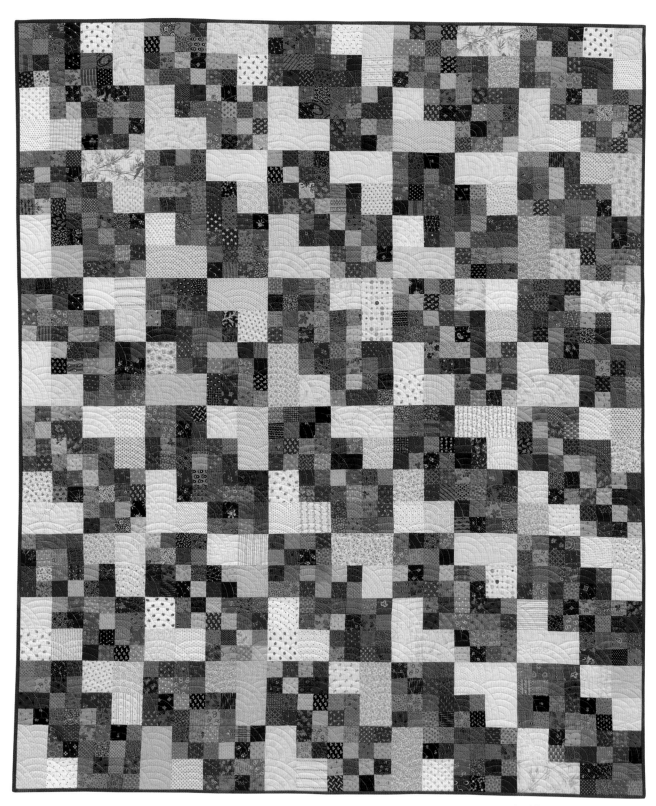

*Quilted by Maggi Honeyman*

## BLOCK 3

**1.** Lay out two A and two D squares in two rows. Sew the squares together to make a four-patch unit. Make 36 units that measure 4½" square, including the seam allowances.

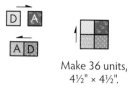

Make 36 units,
4½" × 4½".

**2.** Lay out two step 1 units and two A units as shown to make a pink diagonal chain. Sew the units together into rows. Join the rows to make a unit. Make 18 units that measure 8½" square, including the seam allowances.

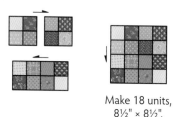

Make 18 units,
8½" × 8½".

**3.** Lay out two step 2 units and two B units in two rows as shown to make a pink diagonal chain. Sew the units together to complete block 3. Make nine blocks that measure 16½" square, including the seam allowances.

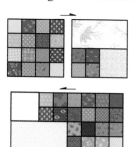
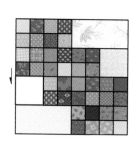

Block 3.
Make 9 blocks,
16½" × 16½".

## BLOCK 4

**1.** Lay out two A and two E squares in two rows. Sew the squares together to make a four-patch unit. Make 24 units that measure 4½" square, including the seam allowances.

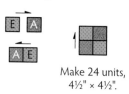

Make 24 units,
4½" × 4½".

**2.** Lay out two step 1 units and two A units as shown to make a blue diagonal chain. Sew the units together into rows. Join the rows to make a unit. Make 12 units that measure 8½" square, including the seam allowances.

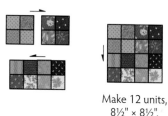

Make 12 units,
8½" × 8½".

**3.** Lay out two step 2 units and two B units in two rows as shown to make a blue diagonal chain. Sew the units together to complete block 4. Make six blocks that measure 16½" square, including the seam allowances.

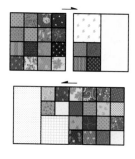
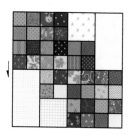

Block 4.
Make 6 blocks,
16½" × 16½".

**1.** Lay out two A and two F squares in two rows. Join the squares to make a four-patch unit. Make 32 units that measure 4½" square, including the seam allowances.

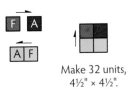

Make 32 units,
4½" × 4½".

**2.** Join two step 1 units and two A units as shown to make a purple diagonal chain. Make eight units that measure 8½" square, including the seam allowances.

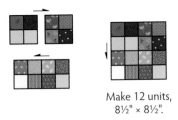

Make 12 units,
8½" × 8½".

**3.** Lay out two step 2 units and two B units as shown to make a purple diagonal chain. Join the units to complete block 5. Make four blocks that measure 16½" square, including the seam allowances.

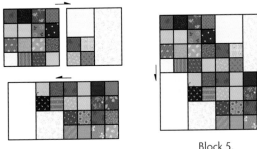

Block 5.
Make 4 blocks,
16½" × 16½".

## Assembling the Quilt Top

**1.** Lay out the blocks in six rows of five blocks each as shown below. Sew the blocks together into rows. Join the rows to complete the quilt top. The quilt top should measure 80½" × 96½".

**2.** Stitch around the perimeter of the quilt top, ⅛" from the outer edges, to lock the seams in place.

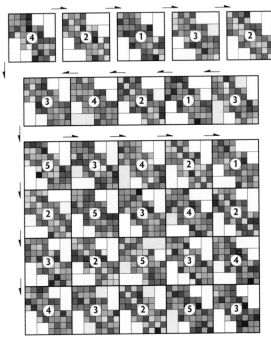

Quilt assembly

## Finishing the Quilt

For more details on any of the finishing steps, go to ShopMartingale.com/HowtoQuilt to download free illustrated information.

**1.** Layer the backing, batting, and quilt top; baste.

**2.** Hand or machine quilt. The quilt shown is machine quilted with a Baptist fan motif of evenly spaced arcs.

**3.** Sew the dark red 2½"-wide strips together end to end with 45° seams to make the binding. Fold this long strip in half lengthwise with wrong sides together and press. Use the long strip to bind the quilt.

## Swatch Cards

I combined scraps of reproduction prints from many different fabric designers and collections for this quilt. So the swatches are less about any particular color and more about the fabric genre and balancing the number of pieces of each color.

## Alternate Colorway

Notice how this quilt pattern works equally as well in an entirely different color palette, such as the pastels shown here. Picture it in 1930s reproduction prints for a sweet little girl or a guest bedroom.

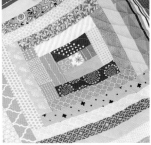

# Kismet

Looking at colors and fabrics through other people's eyes is one of the best ways to break out of your color comfort zone, or CCZ for short. When I decided to tackle writing this book, I thought it would be fun to ask a few friends if they'd be open to create color options. The prolific Melissa Corry created a bright version of my Courthouse Steps pattern, which I'm happily featuring here. It's truly kismet!

**FINISHED QUILT: 74" × 92⅜"  |  FINISHED BLOCK: 13" × 13"**

## Materials

*Yardage is based on 42"-wide fabric.*

+ 4½ yards *total* of assorted blue prints for blocks (A)

+ 4½ yards *total* of assorted green prints for blocks (B)

+ ¾ yard of navy solid for binding

+ 5⅔ yards of fabric for backing

+ 82" × 101" piece of batting

## Cutting

**From the A fabrics, cut a *total* of:**
56 rectangles, 1½" × 13½"
80 rectangles, 1½" × 11½"
80 rectangles, 1½" × 9½"
80 rectangles, 1½" × 7½"
80 rectangles, 1½" × 5½"
80 rectangles, 1½" × 3½"
60 squares, 1½" × 1½"

**From the B fabrics, cut a *total* of:**
16 rectangles, 1½" × 15½"
40 rectangles, 1½" × 13½"
80 rectangles, 1½" × 11½"
80 rectangles, 1½" × 9½"
80 rectangles, 1½" × 7½"
80 rectangles, 1½" × 5½"
80 rectangles, 1½" × 3½"
60 squares, 1½" × 1½"

**From the navy solid, cut:**
9 strips, 2½" × 42"

## Making Block 1

Press the seam allowances in the directions indicated by the arrows. In block 1, the center square will be blue, as will all horizontal strips. The vertical strips will be green.

**1.** Sew B squares to both sides of an A square. Sew 1½" × 3½" A rectangles to the top and bottom of the unit. Make 20 units that measure 3½" square, including the seam allowances.

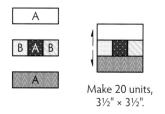

Make 20 units, 3½" × 3½".

**2.** Sew fabric B 1½" × 3½" rectangles to opposite sides of a step 1 unit. Sew 1½" × 5½" fabric A rectangles to the top and bottom of the unit. Make 20 units that measure 5½" square, including the seam allowances.

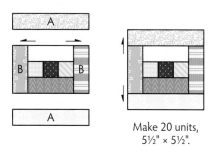

Make 20 units, 5½" × 5½".

**3.** Continue adding fabric B and then fabric A rectangles as shown, ending with 1½" × 13½" fabric A rectangles. Make 20 blocks that measure 13½" square, including the seam allowances.

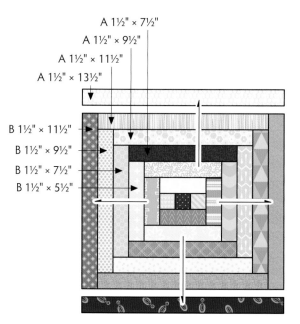

A 1½" × 7½"
A 1½" × 9½"
A 1½" × 11½"
A 1½" × 13½"

B 1½" × 11½"
B 1½" × 9½"
B 1½" × 7½"
B 1½" × 5½"

Block 1.
Make 20 blocks,
13½" × 13½".

Made and quilted by Melissa Corry

## Making Block 2

In block 2, the color placement is the opposite of block 1.

**1.** Sew A squares to both sides of a B square. Sew 1½" × 3½" B rectangles to the top and bottom of the unit. Make 20 units that measure 3½" square, including the seam allowances.

Make 20 units, 3½" × 3½".

**2.** Sew 1½" × 3½" A rectangles to opposite sides of a step 1 unit. Sew 1½" × 5½" B rectangles to the top and bottom of the unit. Make 20 units that measure 5½" square, including the seam allowances.

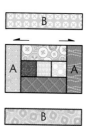
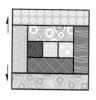

Make 20 units, 5½" × 5½".

**3.** Continue adding fabric A and then fabric B rectangles as shown, ending with 1½" × 13½" fabric B rectangles. Make 20 blocks that measure 13½" square, including the seam allowances.

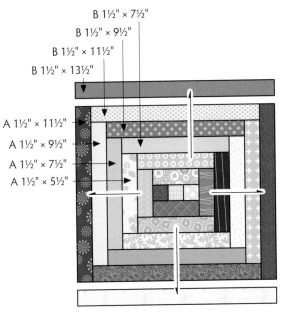

B 1½" × 7½"
B 1½" × 9½"
B 1½" × 11½"
B 1½" × 13½"

A 1½" × 11½"
A 1½" × 9½"
A 1½" × 7½"
A 1½" × 5½"

Block 2.
Make 20 blocks, 13½" × 13½".

## Making the Setting Triangles

**1.** Add one more round of strips to eight of the block 2s, adding 1½" × 13½" fabric A strips to the sides and then 1½" × 15½" fabric B strips to the top and bottom to make eight blocks that are 15½" square.

**2.** For the top and bottom setting triangles, cut three blocks in half diagonally from the upper-right to lower-left corner to make six triangles.

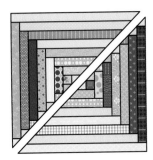

Cut 6 triangles.

**3.** For the side setting triangles, cut four blocks in half diagonally from the upper-left to lower-right corner to make eight triangles.

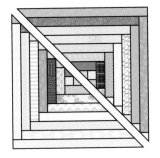

Cut 8 triangles.

**4.** For the corner triangles, cut one block into quarters diagonally to make four triangles.

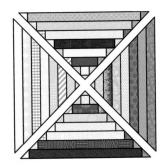

Cut 4 triangles.

## Scrap-Quilt Ready

When you look at the cutting list, you may faint at seeing all of the 1½"-wide strips and pieces that are called for. But an easy way to be scrap-quilt ready is to cut a 1½"-wide strip off of every new fabric you buy when you are squaring up the yardage to begin cutting your current project. Store all of your 1½"-wide strips together, and before you know it, you'll be on your way to a scrappy Log Cabin or Courthouse Steps quilt.

## Assembling the Quilt Top

**1.** Lay out the blocks and the setting triangles as shown in the quilt assembly diagram below. Sew the blocks and side triangles together into diagonal rows. Join the rows and add the corner triangles last to complete the quilt top.

**2.** Square up the edges of the quilt top and then stitch around the perimeter of the quilt top, ⅛" from the outer edges, to lock the seams in place.

## Finishing the Quilt

For more details on any of the finishing steps, go to ShopMartingale.com/HowtoQuilt to download free illustrated information.

**1.** Layer the backing, batting, and quilt top; baste.

**2.** Hand or machine quilt. The quilt shown is machine quilted with wavy horizontal lines.

**3.** Sew the navy 2½"-wide strips together end to end with 45° seams to make the binding. Fold this long strip in half lengthwise with wrong sides together and press. Use the long strip to bind the quilt.

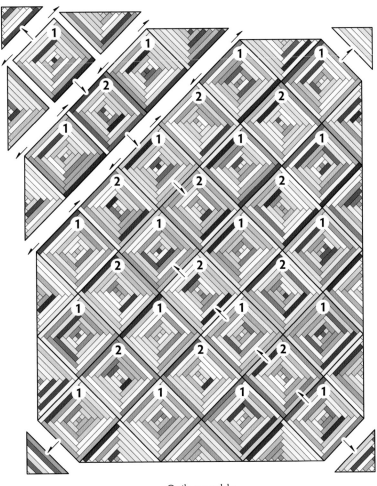

Quilt assembly

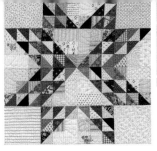

# Firecrackers

Not all quilts are made in a day, and Firecrackers certainly fits *that* bill. However, even for a quilt like this with hundreds of pieces, I still like to do a bit of mindless sewing at the end of the day. After all, as the mother of five, it's my therapy! The instructions below are written for traditionally piecing all the half-square-triangle units in the quilt. However, I used Cake Mix triangle papers, which are designed to perfectly fit on 10" Layer Cake squares to maximize your fabric use. See the tip on page 82 if you're planning to use Layer Cakes too.

**FINISHED QUILT: 80½" × 80½"  |  FINISHED BLOCK: 24" × 24"**

## Materials

*Yardage is based on 42"-wide fabric.*

+ 6½ yards *total* of assorted light prints for blocks and border (A)
+ 2⅞ yards *total* of assorted red and blue prints for blocks and border (B)
+ ¾ yard of blue print for binding
+ 7½ yards of fabric for backing
+ 89" × 89" piece of batting

## Cutting

**From the A fabrics, cut a *total* of:**
12 strips, 2½" × 24½"
36 squares, 6½" × 6½"
108 rectangles, 2½" × 4½"
402 squares, 2⅞" × 2⅞"
108 squares, 2½" × 2½"

**From the B fabrics, cut a *total* of:**
402 squares, 2⅞" × 2⅞"
4 squares, 2½" × 2½"

**From the blue print, cut:**
9 strips, 2½" × 42"

*Quilted by Maggi Honeyman*

## Making the Blocks

Press the seam allowances in the directions indicated by the arrows.

**1.** Layer a 2⅞" A square on top of a 2⅞" B square, right sides together. Draw a diagonal line from corner to corner on the top square. Sew ¼" from each side of the marked line. Cut the units apart on the marked line to make two half-square-triangle units. Make a total of 804 units that measure 2½" square.

Make 804 units,
2½" × 2½".

**2.** Lay out six half-square-triangle units, one 2½" A square, and one A rectangle in three rows as shown. Sew the pieces together into rows. Join the rows to make a unit. Make 108 units that measure 6½" square. Set aside the remaining half-square-triangle units for the triangle border.

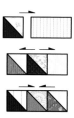 

Make 108 units,
6½" × 6½".

**3.** Lay out 12 units from step 2 and four 6½" A squares in four rows as shown. Sew the pieces together into rows. Join the rows to complete block 1. Make three blocks that measure 24½" square, including the seam allowances.

**4.** Repeat step 3 to make one of block 2, three of block 3, and two of block 4.

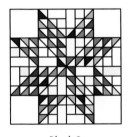

Block 2.
Make 1 block,
24½" × 24½".

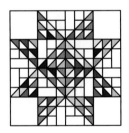

Block 3.
Make 3 blocks,
24½" × 24½".

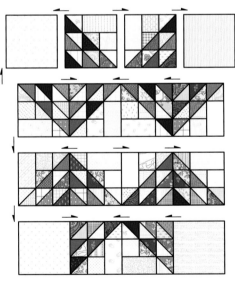

Block 1.
Make 3 blocks,
24½" × 24½".

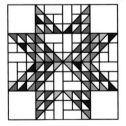

Block 4.
Make 2 blocks,
24½" × 24½".

## Yum—Try a Cake Mix!

If the thought of cutting hundreds of small squares and marking diagonal lines on them makes your head reel, there's another way. Start with a pile of 10" fabric squares (Layer Cakes) and layer two of them at a time with a sheet of Cake Mix paper on top. Then simply sew on the solid lines as instructed and cut apart on the dashed lines. One package of Cake Mix Recipe 3 papers is enough to make 810 half-square-triangle units that are exactly the size you need for this quilt.

**1.** Layer two squares right sides together with the darker fabric on the bottom.

**2.** Pin the paper pattern on top, with the pins in the margins so you don't sew over them.

**3.** Sew on the solid lines, following the arrows. You can finish sewing all lines in one fell swoop without stopping except to pivot when you reach a corner.

**4.** Press the completed squares to set the thread.

**5.** Cut apart on the dashed lines using a rotary cutter and ruler. Leave the paper attached.

**6.** Press the resulting units from the fabric side. Flip the darker fabric open and press it flat. See that? The seam allowance will always be pressed toward the dark fabric!

**7.** Remove the paper before you sew the half-square-triangle units into your quilt. They're already trimmed to the perfect size.

## Making the Triangle Border

**1.** Lay out 38 half-square-triangle units, making sure to orient the units as shown. Join the units to make a side border. Make two borders that measure 2½" × 76½", including the seam allowances.

Make 2 borders, 2½" × 76½".

**2.** Lay out 40 half-square-triangle units, making sure to orient the units as shown. Join the units to make the top border. Repeat to make the bottom border. The borders should measure 2½" × 80½", including the seam allowances.

Make 2 borders, 2½" × 80½".

## Assembling the Quilt Top

**1.** Lay out the blocks, 2½" × 24½" A strips, and 2½" B squares in rows as shown in the quilt assembly diagram below. Sew the pieces together into rows. Join the rows to complete the quilt-top center. The quilt top should measure 76½" square, including the seam allowances.

**2.** Sew the borders to the sides first, and then the top and bottom of the quilt top, making sure the B triangle bases adjoin the quilt top. The quilt top should measure 80½" square.

**3.** Stitch around the perimeter of the quilt top, ⅛" from the outer edges, to lock the seams in place.

## Finishing the Quilt

For more details on any of the finishing steps, go to ShopMartingale.com/HowtoQuilt to download free illustrated information.

**1.** Layer the backing, batting, and quilt top; baste.

**2.** Hand or machine quilt. The quilt shown is machine quilted with curved lines and large and small feather motifs in the triangles.

**3.** Sew the blue 2½"-wide strips together end to end with 45° seams to make the binding. Fold this long strip in half lengthwise with wrong sides together and press. Use the long strip to bind the quilt.

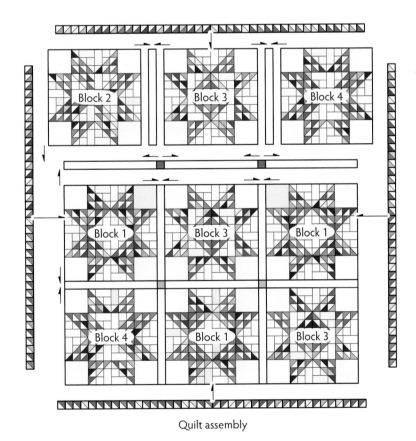

Quilt assembly

# Indian Blanket

While some quiltmakers shy away from triangles, this quilt contains nothing *but* them. You've got to admit, nothing but triangles makes for a spectacular achievement. If you're not already a master of triangles, you surely will be by the time you've completed this quilt. While I used a limited color palette, the most important aspect of this design is the value placement, so take care in sorting your dark, medium, and light prints before you begin. And toss in some brights for a little bit of zing!

**FINISHED QUILT: 57" × 57"**

## Materials

*Yardage is based on 42"-wide fabric.*

+ 2⅛ yards *total* of assorted darks prints (blues and grays) for units (A)
+ ⅞ yards *total* of assorted medium prints (yellows) for units (B)
+ 2⅝ yards *total* of assorted light prints (creams, light blues, and light grays) for units (C)
+ ¼ yard *total* of assorted bright prints (corals and cheddars) for units (D)
+ ⅝ yard of bright print for binding
+ 3½ yards of fabric for backing
+ 63" × 63" piece of batting

## Cutting

*See "Triangle Squares" on page 88 before cutting.*

**From the A fabrics, cut a *total* of:**
310 squares, 2⅞" × 2⅞"; cut 40 of the squares in half diagonally to yield 80 triangles

**From the B fabrics, cut a *total* of:**
113 squares, 2⅞" × 2⅞"

**From the C fabrics, cut a *total* of:**
390 squares, 2⅞" × 2⅞"

**From the D fabrics, cut a *total* of:**
13 squares, 2⅞" × 2⅞"

**From the bright print, cut:**
7 strips, 2½" × 42"

## Making the Half-Square-Triangle Units

Press the seam allowances in the directions indicated by the arrows.

**1.** Using 268 A and 268 C squares, layer a C square on top of each A square, right sides together. Draw a diagonal line from corner to corner on the top square. Sew ¼" from each side of the marked line. Cut the units apart on the marked line to make two half-square-triangle units. Trim the units to measure 2½" square. Make a total of 536 of unit 1.

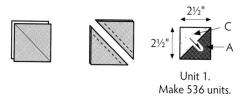

Unit 1.
Make 536 units.

**2.** Repeat step 1 using 112 B and 112 C squares to make 224 of unit 2.

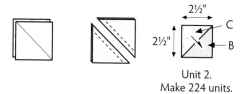

Unit 2.
Make 224 units.

**3.** Use 10 C and 10 D squares to make 20 of unit 3.

Unit 3.
Make 20 units,
2½" × 2½".

**4.** Use two A and two D squares to make four of unit 4.

Unit 4.
Make 4 units,
2½" × 2½".

**5.** Use one B and one D square to make two of unit 5.

Unit 5.
Make 2 units,
2½" × 2½".

## Triangle Squares

We all have our favorite way to make triangle squares or half-square-triangle units. I like to mark a diagonal line on a square, sew on both sides of the line, and cut the pieces apart on the diagonal to yield two units. If you like to have a bit of excess fabric so you can trim and square up your units after making each one, cut 3" squares rather than 2⅞" squares. With so many triangle squares in one quilt, squaring them up before assembling the quilt top is not a bad idea!

## Assembling the Quilt Top

**1.** Referring to the diagram at right, lay out 134 of unit 1, 56 of unit 2, and 20 A triangles in 20 rows to form one quadrant of the quilt. Place all units so the blue, gray, and yellow triangles point toward the inner corner (or bottom-right corner as oriented here). For interest, replace four to ten of the units in the layout with units 3, 4, and 5. (You'll have a total of 26 of these units with D fabrics to use throughout all four quadrants.)

**2.** Sew the units and triangles together into rows. Join the rows to make one section. Make four sections.

Make 4.

**3.** Lay out the four sections, rotating them as shown in the quilt assembly diagram below. Join the sections to complete the quilt top, which should measure 57" square.

**4.** Stitch around the perimeter of the quilt top, ⅛" from the outer edges, to lock the seams in place.

## Finishing the Quilt

For more details on any of the finishing steps, go to ShopMartingale.com/HowtoQuilt to download free illustrated information.

**1.** Layer the backing, batting, and quilt top; baste.

**2.** Hand or machine quilt. The quilt shown is machine quilted with petals and a feather motif.

**3.** Sew the bright 2½"-wide strips together end to end with 45° seams to make the binding. Fold this long strip in half lengthwise with wrong sides together and press. Use the long strip to bind the quilt.

Quilt assembly

# Friendship Blues

This quilt may be the last one in the book, but it's the quilt that inspired the entire book. While I'm fortunate to have lots of scraps, I decided to ask my friends to send me a 5" square of blue fabric. Maggi Honeyman, who quilts many of my quilts, sent me a vintage piece. Tammy Vonderschmitt sent me a handful of some of her blue scraps. I included a few pieces of my mother's clothing as a remembrance of her, since she had recently passed away. I took all these treasured scraps and tied them into one quilt that tells a story of friends and memories—a real treasure!

**FINISHED QUILT: 84⅜" × 84⅜"  |  FINISHED BLOCK: 4" × 4"**

## Materials

*Yardage is based on 42"-wide fabric.*

+ 6½ yards *total* of assorted dark blue prints for blocks, setting triangles, and border (A)
+ 1⅝ yards *total* of assorted light prints for blocks (B)
+ ¾ yard of blue print for binding
+ 7¾ yards of fabric for backing
+ 93" × 93" piece of batting

## Cutting

**From the A fabrics, cut a *total* of:**
8½"-wide strips to total 315" (can be 1 print or assorted prints)
11 squares, 7" × 7"; cut each square into quarters diagonally to yield 44 side triangles
121 squares, 4½" × 4½"
2 squares, 4" × 4"; cut each square in half diagonally to yield 4 corner triangles
288 squares, 2½" × 2½" (144 sets of 2 matching squares)

**From the B fabrics, cut a *total* of:**
288 squares, 2½" × 2½" (144 sets of 2 matching squares)

**From the blue print, cut:**
9 strips, 2½" × 42"

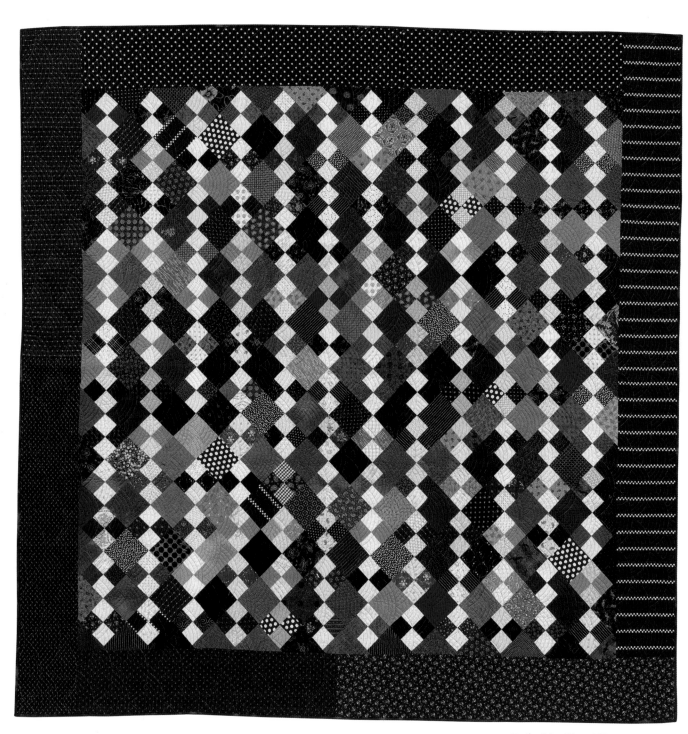

*Quilted by Maggi Honeyman*

## Making the Blocks

Press the seam allowances in the directions indicated by the arrows.

Lay out two matching A squares and two matching B squares in two rows. Sew the squares together into rows. Join the rows to make a Four Patch block. Make a total of 144 blocks that measure 4½" square.

Make 144 blocks,
4½" × 4½".

### What Color Do You See?

Did you know that men and women see color differently? If you shop with a girlfriend for a red dress, she's more likely to favor one that's a bluish-red, like cherry red. Shop with a man, and he's more likely to choose the red-orange or tomato red.

To help when laying out your blocks, squint at the layout to see if any fabrics clash or stick out. They don't all need to be the same shade of blue, but rearrange them until the ones that seem to clash are next to a different and more pleasing hue.

## Family Reunion Quilt

Does your family gather for reunions? They're a perfect opportunity to ask for fabric donations for a family quilt. The four patches in this quilt are large enough for little hands to help, and there's room to autograph the light squares.

## Assembling the Quilt Top

**1.** Lay out the blocks, 4½" A squares, and the A side and corner triangles in diagonal rows. Sew the blocks, squares, and side triangles into rows. Join the rows and add the corner triangles last. Trim and square up the quilt top, making sure to leave ¼" beyond the points of all the blocks for seam allowances. The quilt top should measure 68⅜" square.

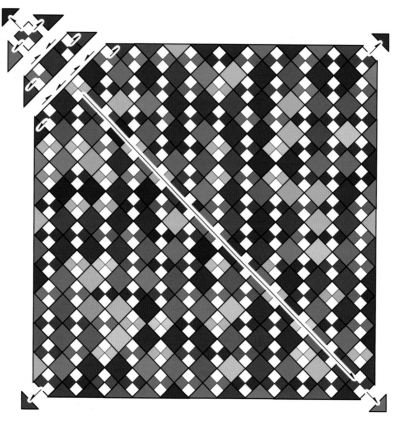

Quilt assembly

**2.** Sew the 8½"-wide A strips together end to end using a straight seam. From the pieced strip, cut two 68⅜"-long strips and two 84⅜"-long strips. Sew the 68⅜"-long strips to opposite sides of the quilt top. Sew the 84⅜"-long strips to the top and bottom of the quilt top to complete the border. The quilt should measure 84⅜" square.

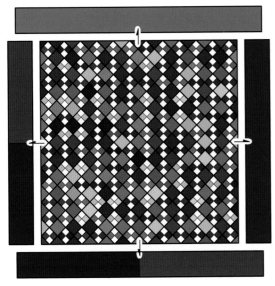

Adding borders

## Finishing the Quilt

For more details on any of the finishing steps, go to ShopMartingale.com/HowtoQuilt to download free illustrated information.

**1.** Layer the backing, batting, and quilt top; baste.

**2.** Hand or machine quilt. The quilt shown is machine quilted with an allover Baptist Fan motif.

**3.** Sew the blue 2½"-wide strips together end to end with 45° seams to make the binding. Fold this long strip in half lengthwise with wrong sides together and press. Use the long strip to bind the quilt.

## Baptist Fan Quilting

Did you notice the quilting on this quilt? It's an allover fan pattern, commonly known as the Baptist fan. Maggi Honeyman did the quilting and I love how the curved lines of her stitching provide a nice counterpoint to the squares and angles in the patchwork.

When a quilt is filled with dense color and a simple patchwork pattern, an allover quilting motif often works best. I think Maggi's choice is a perfect ending to this treasured friendship quilt.

## Alternate Colorway

To make this friendship quilt, I thought it would be easy to ask everyone to send me a blue fabric, knowing I could make all of the blues play nice together. But that's not to say you couldn't make this pattern from a wider variety of colors. Spread the colors around, and include a couple of brights to give some punch to the final design.

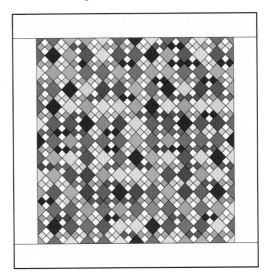

# About the Author

### Why *Oh, Scrap!?*

I've had a crazy, amazing life, a wild journey that I could never have imagined. Through it all, I've learned to take the pieces and stitch them together to make something new. My life is a patchwork of family, friends, and people who have made an impact.

My quilting story is a simple one. The first quilt I made was for a wedding gift. My sister and I worked on it together. It was a quilt-as-you-go project that we mailed back-and-forth between Lubbock and Dallas. It's clear that I was destined to be a scrap quilter because my next quilt was made from a sampler pack of a thousand 1½" squares. (I thought the finished quilt would be bigger.) My next quilt was made from "reading" the pictures in a Japanese magazine. I didn't realize the measurements were all metric, so needless to say the second quilt was huge. You could say I am self-taught and continue to learn as I go.

The rest of my story is still a work in progress. It started with that first wedding quilt and led to working in a quilt shop. I raised kids and now I'm blessed with grandchildren. I am part of an industry and community of people who share my love for quilts and the people who make them.

To everyone reading this...thank you for being part of my scrappy story.